God and Other Things

Conversations That Defend Faith, Question Evolution, and Search for Truth

Wade Winingham

ISBN: 0-6156-7497-6
ISBN-13: 9780615674971

Thanks and Dedication

God and Other Things was written for my children: Matt, Laura, and Megan. I love them all.

I would like to thank my wife Marcia for her comments on all of the revisions, and for her unfailing encouragement throughout the long process.

God and Other Things is dedicated to the memory of my father, Jim Winingham, who taught me to treasure good books and lively conversation. He challenged me to defend myself whenever we disagreed, which was often. Sometimes I won.

***

Table of Contents

Introduction

I want you to know what to expect when you read this book, so let me tell you what I had in mind when I wrote it. I wanted to show that you don't have to be stupid or dim-witted to be a Christian. I wanted to show that defending your beliefs is worthwhile. And I wanted to show that intelligent people can disagree without attacking each other. Really, it can be done.

You will find many questions in this book, such as:

- Is God even necessary today?
- Isn't the only truth that there is no absolute truth?
- Didn't Darwin kill God with science?
- Was Jesus really God, or just a great teacher?
- Isn't the New Testament full of contradictions?
- Aren't Christians arrogant about their God?
- Why does a loving God allow human suffering?
- How can God send good people to Hell?

What you will not find in this book is a single footnote or scriptural reference. I have no prejudice against footnotes or scripture, but they can turn a friendly chat into a tedious lecture. This book is a conversation, and conversations should move along quickly. You can move through this book quickly.

Some of you will not agree with the opinions expressed in this book. A few of them border on heresy, I suppose, but I take comfort in the fact that burning at the stake went out of style years ago. Please read the book with an open mind, and remember that my intention was to stimulate thought and discussion, not to offend.

My hope is that you have fun reading God and Other Things, and that it will encourage you to look further into the mystery and joy of faith in God.

Wade Winingham. 2012.
***

Someone Is Out There

PAUL: So tell me. Are you still searching for the "Meaning of Life?" Your divine purpose?

KAREN: Of course. How do you manage to go through life if you don't know why you're here?

PAUL: Why don't you just relax? Drink your coffee. Eat a bagel. Enjoy the company of an entertaining friend. You spend too much time analyzing yourself.

KAREN: Maybe. But I can't live like a lot of our friends—entirely self-absorbed but not at all self-reflective. You remember what Socrates said, "An unexamined life is not worth living."

PAUL: That's just like you. We haven't been here five minutes, and you have me arguing with a dead Greek. You ought to give that poor old guy a rest. And yourself. Why don't you just enjoy life instead of digging around for your own personal meaning? You may be searching for something that can't be found. What's the point?

KAREN: Well, that's the question, isn't it? "What is the point?" The point of life, I mean. What can be more important than finding the purpose of your existence? It can't be just to work and eat and sleep and watch television.

PAUL: It depends on if you have cable.

KAREN: That makes it more bearable, I admit. But working toward your purpose in life is the main point of life. Everything else is either survival or distraction. I can't believe you're so shallow that you don't wonder about such things.

PAUL: Oh, I wonder. And I've searched a bit myself, but I suspect we have ended up in different places. Sometimes I think Mark Twain got it right. He said, "Good friends, good books, and a sleepy conscience. This is the ideal life." Maybe that's all there is.

KAREN: Enjoying those three is part of my purpose. Yours too, I know. But I'm looking for something more.

PAUL: As I recall, your search was leading you toward a sacred being. The one you call God?

KAREN: That seems inevitable.

PAUL: I don't see it as inevitable, or even necessary. It might be more productive to stay away from God and look for meaning a little closer to home.

KAREN: You don't think the search for God is worthwhile?

PAUL: I'm just not sure it's necessary.

KAREN: Is joy necessary? Living life to the fullest? Peace of mind, love, wisdom and understanding? Forgiveness? Acceptance? How necessary are those things to you?

PAUL: Very. But most of those things are in me. I don't see how searching for God is going to help me find them. He is a long way from here, if he's even real, which is doubtful.

KAREN: Most of the world's population disagrees with you on that. That includes me, by the way.

PAUL: I'm sure it does, and I know how you love to debate. But consider yourself warned. I've spent some time investigating this very subject. You'd better not challenge me on it.

KAREN: Don't consider it a challenge. Look at it as a meeting of the minds.

PAUL: Great minds?

KAREN: We'll see.

PAUL: OK. Then let's start with a simple question. Does it really matter if there is a God? How will that make a difference on whether I have cereal for breakfast, or steak and eggs?

KAREN: You consider the existence of God a simple question? The response to that question has shaped most of human history, and still does. As to your choice of breakfast foods, I think it's pretty much left up to you, whether God exists or not. Personally, I'd go with steak every time. Medium rare.

PAUL: I'm with you there. There's nothing like a juicy steak to get you started in the morning. Whether God exists or not. That's the point I'm trying to make. The existence of God makes no difference in daily life.

KAREN: But it makes a difference even to believe that it makes no difference. Your behavior, your opinions, the way you view everything in the world is colored by your concept of God, or no God, or nature worship, or humanism, whatever. I'm amazed that people don't take this more seriously. And I believe you do. You just don't want to admit it. You said you investigated this subject. If it doesn't matter if there is a God, why did you bother?

PAUL: Don't try to draw any grand conclusions about my motives. I was just curious, mostly. Even mystified. I find it amazing that people base their lives on the idea of some kind of god. I mean how they live, how they act, how they eat, sleep, dance, marry, you name it. Western civilization keeps track of time itself in relation to a traveling preacher who died in the Middle East two thousand years ago.

KAREN: So your alarm clock has a picture of Jesus on it?

PAUL: I'm talking about our calendar. Year Number One started when Jesus was born. Or at least when everybody says he was born. Why pick the birth of Jesus as the starting point for keeping track of time? Doesn't that strike you as strange?

KAREN: I suppose a calendar has to start somewhere. The arrival of God in human form seems like as good a place as any. What would you choose, the day they invented frozen pizza?

PAUL: Do not mock frozen pizza. Some of my best memories include the taste of imitation cheese and mysterious meats on a crispy crust. I'm just saying it may not be a good idea to make God so important. Look what it leads to. History is full of religious fanatics dancing over bloody corpses.

KAREN: I guess I missed that picture in the World History textbook.

PAUL: Maybe you weren't paying attention during our discussion about the Crusades.

KAREN: I remember the discussion.

PAUL: Good. Then you remember how your priests burned men alive. Cut them to pieces for heresy. Cut their heads off. Tortured them. Then there were the Puritans. They liked fire too. They burned teenage girls as witches. Even the Mormons slaughtered wagons full of people to keep them out of their territory. All this in the name of God. It's crazy.

KAREN: That stuff is crazy. I'll give you that. But history books aren't known for giving a balanced view of religion.

PAUL: Probably not. But there are other sources. You would be surprised how much information is out there.

KAREN: Some of it is probably even true. What else did you find floating around in this sea of information?

PAUL: I found more questions than answers. Frankly, I was surprised to find myths about God as far back as cave men. It seems that ever since humans crawled up out of the swamp, they've been trying to find God. Or at least something to worship.

KAREN: I'll pass on the swamp illustration for a moment. What do you make of all this searching for God? Why did it happen?

PAUL: I wonder if people just enjoy a good story. You know, they like to sit around the campfire and swap tall tales. Like Paul Bunyan, or Superman.

KAREN: You're trying to equate Superman with God? I'm beginning to doubt your sincerity.

PAUL: You don't think God dresses in blue tights and leaps tall buildings in a single bound?

KAREN: I think you are avoiding the subject.

PAUL: It's a big subject.

KAREN: It's the biggest. That's what makes it worth the effort.

PAUL: You're not going to let this drop, are you?

KAREN: You started it. And I would like an answer. Why do you think people have always searched for God?

PAUL: The only thing I can figure is there must be some deep-seated need in humans for more to life than what we can see or touch. We need to believe in something bigger than ourselves. Something outside ourselves.

KAREN: There may be hope for you yet. If we feel such a need for something, doesn't that tell you it exists?

PAUL: Not necessarily. Somebody once said, "If there was no God, man would create one." Get it? God doesn't exist just because we wish he did. When I was little, I wanted a pony for Christmas, but I didn't get one.

KAREN: But a pony existed. You didn't feel a need for something that wasn't real. How could you? You wanted a pony because there were ponies. You said there is a deep-seated need in us to believe in something. How can that be if the something isn't real?

PAUL: So there are no such things as daydreams? Fantasies? Everything we desire must be achievable?

KAREN: I didn't say it must be achievable. I said it must be real.

PAUL: That seems a rather fine distinction. If I couldn't get the pony, it didn't matter if it was real. My wish for it was based on unrealistic expectations.

KAREN: It may not have been a realistic wish, but it was still a wish for something real. You can't crave something that doesn't exist. Common sense should tell you that.

PAUL: Common sense tells me I didn't get the pony, no matter how badly I wanted it. It didn't happen. Maybe God is like that. Maybe we want him just because we want him. Not because he's really there.

KAREN: I don't buy that. You can't want something that doesn't exist. What other need can you think of that doesn't have some real object? When you get hungry, there is food to eat. When you need affection, there is love. We search for God because God is real. And you need to get over this pony thing.

PAUL: I may be scarred for life. But you're picking examples that are too easy. What about the desire for world peace? Any girl who ever walked down a beauty contest runway wanted that. How much world peace have you seen lately? It seems to me those girls are looking for something that can't exist.

KAREN: I don't know that it can't exist. It probably can and has existed for periods of time. But it seems to me it is a little like hoping for peace and quiet on a grade school playground. You might have it for short periods, but sooner or later somebody is going to pull somebody's hair. And then it's on.

PAUL: I remember how it was on. You were pretty tough for a little girl with a ponytail.

KAREN: And I didn't like to have it pulled. But that's the way of the world, isn't it? Somebody is always pulling somebody's hair, and then a fight starts. But that doesn't prove that peace can't exist. It just proves that it is difficult to achieve. We know peace is real because we've seen it at one time or another, so we crave it. Just like we crave God.

PAUL: I'm afraid you are deluding yourself. Maybe we're just looking for some cosmic Daddy to pat us on the head when we stumble. Then the need for God has no real object. It is insecurity turned into religion.

KAREN: If God offered only comfort and peace, I might agree with you. In fact, that sounds a lot like the modern concept of God many people claim to believe. It is a warm, fuzzy, vague spirit in the sky that demands nothing and accepts everything. That is the kind of God somebody would make up. But the view of God in Christianity, Judaism, or Islam is more personal. That view spells out pretty clearly that this life will be full of pain and trouble, most of it caused by our disobedience to God. That doesn't sound like a human invention to me. It sounds like reality.

PAUL: But that version of reality could be an illusion. Not everybody believes it. Not everybody wants that kind of God.

KAREN: There are no *versions* of reality. Something is either real or it is not.

PAUL: I don't know about that. If you asked the President of United States what it's like to live in Washington D. C., his story would be completely different than somebody who lives in a cardboard box under a bridge, but both versions would be true.

KAREN: That's a good illustration. But the two versions don't contradict each other the way those two versions of God do.

PAUL: Living in a palace and living in a box aren't contradictory?

KAREN: They are different, but they only contradict each other if they can't both be true. Both of the circumstances you describe can be true, unlike the two versions of God.

PAUL: Whichever version you like, you have to agree that not everyone needs God. Not everybody is searching for him.

KAREN: Not everyone admits to it. But everybody has some sense of longing in their lives—a small void that needs to be filled. Some try to fill it with money, some with alcohol, some with endless relationships, whatever. But the point is, you can't fill that emptiness unless you fill it with what is supposed to be there.

PAUL: And that is God?

KAREN: That is what I believe. After all, God is love. Who doesn't want love?

PAUL: You sound like a girl.

KAREN: How perceptive. I am a girl. But even big tough guys like you need love.

PAUL: I may need love, but that doesn't mean I need God. And your theory may be emotional fluff. Just because you want God to be real, that doesn't mean he is. That sounds like wishful thinking to me.

KAREN: If you can give me an example of desiring something that isn't real, I'll concede the point.

PAUL: That's easy. I want to have dinner tonight with Marie Antoinette. How are you going to make that real?

KAREN: Bad example. You wished for something that's impossible, but not unreal. There really was a Marie Antoinette. I think she liked to eat cake.

PAUL: Yeah, but she lost her appetite rather suddenly. Let's say I want to be President. What about that?

KAREN: Wrong again. Your chances of landing in the Oval Office are pretty slim, I'll grant you, but there is a President, isn't there? Your desire is for something difficult, but real.

PAUL: How about this? I want to take a ride with Santa Claus.

KAREN: Santa Claus is a fictional character.

PAUL: Gotcha. I want it, but it isn't real. God could be the same thing. Just a pleasant fiction. I think I just won the argument.

KAREN: This isn't an argument. It is an enlightening conversation. But I think your reasoning is a little off again. If you want to co-pilot for Santa Claus, that doesn't prove you can desire something that isn't real, it proves you need therapy. You know Santa Claus isn't real, so you can't want it and remain sane.

PAUL: Does that mean anybody who believes in God is crazy?

KAREN: I think it means you shouldn't include nonsense in a rational discussion. The fact remains that you can't reasonably desire something that doesn't exist. And every culture in history has searched for God, whether they used that name or not. God must, therefore, exist.

PAUL: I'll concede there have always been God myths. Creator myths. Resurrection myths. Every culture in history has had some kind of God story. We look at them now as silly. If the ancient myths weren't true, why should I believe yours?

KAREN: You seem to think that since different cultures had different God stories, they must all be untrue and there must be no God. That makes no sense to me. If every culture in history believed in *any* particular object, how could that convince you the object didn't exist? It convinces me of exactly the opposite. Humankind has not been full of neurotic fools searching for something that wasn't there. They searched for God because there is a God to search for. Any other explanation defies logic.

PAUL: I'm surprised a believer would rely on logic.

KAREN: Don't let that surprise you. Faith without logic is mere superstition. Besides, if my beliefs can't stand up to logical questions, they aren't worth much. Truth is not afraid of examination.

PAUL: Then let's examine my original question. Why does it matter if God exists? Why should God mean any more to me than the solar system did to Sherlock Holmes?

KAREN: Pardon me?

PAUL: You have heard of Sherlock Holmes?

KAREN: The greatest detective in literature. I didn't realize he was an astronomer.

PAUL: He wasn't. In fact, he didn't even know that the earth revolved around the sun. His partner Watson was shocked by Holmes' ignorance of the subject. But Holmes said, in effect, "What possible difference can it make to me if the earth revolves around the sun, or even the moon? My work will continue either way." It seems to me the same could be said about God. What possible difference will it make to me if he exists or not?

KAREN: It makes all the difference. For one thing, the existence of God is the only real foundation for ethical behavior. Without God, there is no reason to respect life, and no justification for human rights. Worst of all, there is no hope. Not in this life or through eternity.

PAUL: So without God, "Life is a tale told by an idiot, full of sound and fury, signifying nothing?"

KAREN: Not a bad way to put it. Without God, it's hard for me to see how life can have any meaning. After all, what accomplishment in life is not rendered insignificant by death? And without God, what is left after death?

PAUL: You are getting downright depressing.

KAREN: Life without God is depressing.

PAUL: So I should believe in God because it will make me happy and content?

16

KAREN: I can't guarantee that. I would just say it is hard to be happy and content without belief.

PAUL: But not impossible?

KAREN: I'll admit a lot of people achieve a certain level of happiness without belief in God.

PAUL: Then why bother with it? Why is God even relevant?

KAREN: Because even if you are relatively happy without God, I don't see how an intelligent person can find meaning or purpose in a purely material world. Even Jean-Paul Sartre, the famous existentialist, agreed with that. He said atheism is a hard long-term business. The bottom line is that knowing God can lead to joy and personal fulfillment that no atheist can ever know.

PAUL: Could be. Maybe it takes a stronger person to be an atheist than a believer.

KAREN: That is hardly a selling point for atheism, or a reason to give up the search. I can't conceive of why anyone would not want to find out if there is more to life than the physical world. If there is a God, there are answers to all of life's ultimate questions. Questions about destiny, good versus evil, death, the meaning of life.

PAUL: So if there is a God, life's questions can be answered. Is that why I should believe in God?

KAREN: That is a little like asking why you should believe in love, or compassion, or the cup you hold in your hand. You believe in these things because they're real. I could list many ways you could profit from belief in God, but those are benefits of belief, not justifications. The bottom line is simple. You should believe in God because God is real.

PAUL: There's that logic again.

KAREN: It's a gift.

***

It's Not Fair

PAUL: I don't know how far you can get trying to prove the existence of God with logic. It seems to me you will have to rely on faith more than reason.

KAREN: I like to use a little of both. Maybe I'll throw in some philosophy for good measure.

PAUL: Philosophy can be dangerous for someone like you. You might start to question your own beliefs.

KAREN: You know what Francis Bacon said: "A little philosophy inclines a man's mind to atheism, but depth of philosophy brings a man's mind to religion."

PAUL: Then you had better go deep. If you think you can use philosophy to prove the existence of God, I'm willing to listen.

KAREN: That's good, because I'm going to use you as an example.

PAUL: I'll brace myself.

KAREN: Do you remember the last time we were here at the coffee shop? A man cut in line ahead of us, and you—let's see, how do I put this? You expressed your irritation.

PAUL: Given the circumstances, I don't think that's too surprising.

KAREN: Why not?

PAUL: Because he got ahead of me in line. It doesn't pay to get between me and my caffeine.

KAREN: But there was a woman ahead of him when he cut in line. Did you get angry at her?

PAUL: No, but that's different.

KAREN: Different how?

PAUL: It's different because she didn't do anything wrong. She just happened to be ahead of me in line. What are you driving at?

KAREN: As feeble as the example may be, I'm trying to show there is a standard of right and wrong in the world, and that it points to the existence of God. Cutting in line at a coffee shop may be a minor infraction of the standard, but your reaction shows that the standard of behavior is in you.

PAUL: It must not have been in the guy that cut in line. He got his espresso way before I did.

KAREN: So did the lady that was ahead of him, but you didn't get mad at her. She followed the rules, which she knows like everybody else. Even the guy who cut in line knew he had done the wrong thing. Do you remember the way he kept looking at his watch? He was trying to show us that he was running late, so it was all right for him to break the rules.

PAUL: How does that prove he has some internal moral compass? Maybe it just shows he's a jerk.

KAREN: He probably is, but he still knew he had stepped outside the standards of behavior. He didn't just ignore the standard, he tried to make an excuse for breaking it. That shows me it was in him too.

PAUL: It may show he agreed with your standard, but it doesn't prove the standard is universal. Remember your Shakespeare: "Nothing is good or bad, but thinking makes it so." That's pretty much the Hindu philosophy too, as I understand it. All events are morally neutral. Good and bad are all in your head.

KAREN: Shakespeare and Hindus in the same example. You have talent. But I suspect if you pour a cup of hot coffee on a Hindu's head, his response will be less than neutral, and not just because his scalp burns.

PAUL: Do all your examples involve coffee?

KAREN: Sometimes I use tea. The point is that a lot of people claim to believe everything is morally neutral—that there is no good or bad unless someone judges it so. But they don't really live that belief.

PAUL: You are pretty quick to pass judgment. How do you know they don't?

KAREN: Just watch them. You find out a lot more about people by what they do than what they say.

PAUL: No doubt. So what do you see when you peek through their windows?

KAREN: Metaphorically speaking, of course.

PAUL: Of course.

KAREN: I see people who claim that all morals are artificial constraints. They say there is no right or wrong behavior. But the first time you hurt them or cross their boundaries, their response is, "That's not fair."

PAUL: Again, not too surprising. What would you expect them to say?

KAREN: I'll tell you what I would *not* expect them to say: "Don't worry about hurting me. There really is no right or wrong. You can do whatever you like, and so can I. Nobody can say there is anything wrong with it."

PAUL: Oh, but people do say that.

KAREN: Sure, the prisons are full of them. But the great majority of people don't say it. You hear it occasionally, just like you sometimes hear a frat boy say he doesn't like beer. But that's pretty unusual. It is the same with the concept of fairness, or the universal standard I'm trying to get across to you. People don't deny a standard exists, they just make excuses for breaking it.

PAUL: You give them too much credit. I don't think most people have even given it a thought. Why should they make excuses for violating a standard they haven't even considered?

KAREN: That's the point. They don't have to consider it, any more than they consider breathing. They can't stop breathing, and they can't help feeling they have done something wrong when they do something wrong. So they make excuses to soothe their conscience.

PAUL: What kind of excuses?

KAREN: They were drunk. They were broke. They were tired. The guy they stabbed in the back had it coming. It's always something. Whatever the excuse happens to be, they don't say there is no "fair". Because there is. If there were no moral standard of behavior, there would be no need for excuses. But you hear them all the time. Why do you suppose that is?

PAUL: It's human nature. People naturally try to justify their behavior, but it's more a matter of self-esteem than universal morals. Nobody wants to be ashamed of themselves, so they come up with reasons for their indiscretions.

KAREN: You are proving my point for me. Why would they feel shame unless they understood there is a basic standard of behavior? If all events are morally neutral, why would anybody feel shame about anything?

PAUL: I wonder if shame is just a coping mechanism the group uses to keep individuals in line. The rules of etiquette are the same thing. We made them up to lubricate the social machinery.

KAREN: Rules of etiquette are a human invention. And they lubricate the social machinery, to steal your phrase. But they don't create a standard of behavior any more than road maps create roads. They simply organize and illustrate what is already there.

PAUL: Maybe. But you need to consider other possibilities.

KAREN: Like what?

PAUL: Like etiquette, morals, your universal standard—they are all just artificial rules to intimidate the weak and restrain the strong. We cultivate them to keep the bold among us from taking over the world.

KAREN: I don't know if it's working. It seems to me the bold have pretty much taken over the world.

PAUL: I didn't say it always works. But you can't deny the explanation is reasonable.

KAREN: Not the way I see it. What you describe is a philosophical, artificial human invention that has been accepted by everyone in the world. That's a rather fantastic theory. How could everyone learn these rules of yours?

PAUL: You must be kidding. Your mama sings it to you in the cradle. Teachers build it into their lesson plans. They pound good behavior in you from the time you crawl out of the womb till they lay you in a coffin. Doesn't that show you it is learned behavior?

KAREN: We learn about gravity from parents and teachers too. Does that mean gravity doesn't exist until we hear about it? Look, I don't doubt we learn about morals from the adults around us, and even more how to apply them, but that doesn't negate the fact that the knowledge is built in us. Just like it has been in everyone, in all cultures, everywhere, in every time.

PAUL: You must get worn out jumping to such grand conclusions. You surely don't mean to say the standards of moral behavior have been the same throughout history? We can't agree on moral standards everywhere even now. Look at the evening news. Men strap dynamite to their chests and blow up pizza joints to glorify their god. Is that part of your universal standard?

KAREN: That is an example of the standard being broken. Most people in the world are shocked at such behavior, which proves my point. If there was no universal sense of right and wrong, no one would care.

PAUL: But different cultures have different moral codes. Different times in history saw morals in different ways. How does that fit your theory?

KAREN: There have been differences in moral codes at different times, but I submit that they have been minor. No culture has admired murder, or lying, or stealing, or taking another man's wife.

PAUL: I thought for a moment you were going to rattle off the Ten Commandments.

KAREN: I just gave you a partial list. I don't want to overwhelm you.

PAUL: I appreciate your consideration, but I think I can give you an example that disproves your theory.

KAREN: Let's have it.

PAUL: This should be one you like. What about the Romans throwing the Christians to the lions? That was a pretty good example of mass murder. And the Coliseum was full of peasants screaming for more. You can't say they didn't admire murder. Where was your moral code there?

KAREN: I can't make judgments on the motives of the spectators. Maybe they went along with the crowd out of fear or intimidation. Maybe they rejected the moral standard because they were filled with pain and resentment towards the Romans, and they lashed out at whomever they could. I don't know, but I know there were a lot of people who were repulsed by Roman atrocities. You can't say that the culture as a whole admired that behavior.

PAUL: Maybe they didn't, but you have no evidence that it was some kind of built-in moral standard. Maybe it was just a widely held opinion.

KAREN: If moral law is just opinion, then there is no point in ever worrying about right or wrong, because right and wrong don't exist. Killing six million Jews in the Holocaust is no better or worse than Mother Theresa working with the poor in Calcutta. I don't think you will find many people to agree with that comparison.

PAUL: So this moral sense you're so proud of is a law? Something we have to obey, like natural laws?

KAREN: Not exactly. Water has to freeze at thirty-two degrees. It has no choice but to obey its law. We do have a choice.

PAUL: You are talking about free will.

KAREN: Right. You surely believe in that.

PAUL: Not everybody does. Wasn't it the philosopher Spinoza who said that free will was an illusion? He said our belief in free will made as much sense as a rock thinking it could decide where to land after it was thrown.

KAREN: That is surprisingly coherent for a philosopher.

PAUL: I thought you were a philosopher.

KAREN: Only part time. I communicate too clearly to be entirely in their camp.

PAUL: Do you care to clearly respond to Spinoza?

KAREN: I'll respond. I think he was wrong. Humans are not just a sack full of instincts and predetermined responses. For one thing, animals that live by instinct don't exhibit the trait of self-sacrifice. Humans do.

PAUL: A mama wolf won't give her life for her pups?

KAREN: She probably will. But she won't do it for some other wolf. Humans will.

PAUL: Humans will give their lives for a wolf?

KAREN: You know what I mean. They will give their lives for each other. There are plenty of examples, but let me tell you a short story about that. It took place in 1941 at Auschwitz.

PAUL: The Nazi concentration camp?

KAREN: Right. A prisoner escaped one night, and the Nazi commandant was so mad about it he decided to take it out on the prisoners in the camp. He chose ten men to lock in a concrete bunker, and told them they would stay there till they starved to death. One of the men broke down and started to cry for his wife and children. Just before they walked in the bunker, a Polish priest named Father Kolbe stepped forward and said, "I will take that man's place." Kolbe knew he faced certain death when they slammed the door behind him, but he went in anyway, so another man could live. The man he died for lived to have children and grandchildren because of another man's sacrifice.

PAUL: There were probably a lot of stories like that in the death camps that we never heard, but they prove only that humans are capable of self-sacrifice. There is no way to prove that the behavior was choice rather than an instinct to protect the group.

KAREN: I see no reason to believe that a person would ignore his survival instinct for members of a group that meant nothing to him. Such a group instinct makes no sense to me. Self-sacrificing behavior is not instinct. It is choice. The ability to choose behavior is fundamental to being human. Like having opposable thumbs.

PAUL: Apes have opposable thumbs.

KAREN: I should have known you would catch that one. I'll drop the thumb argument. But I presume you think we are better at making choices than the rock Spinoza liked to toss around?

PAUL: I believe we can choose our behavior, if that's what you mean.

KAREN: That is what I mean.

PAUL: But people frequently choose bad behavior, wouldn't you agree?

KAREN: No question.

PAUL: Then where is your God? If he made us, and planted this moral law in us, why did he allow us to choose evil?

KAREN: How could he not? Free will is freedom to make choices—good or bad. If we could only choose the good and never the bad, we would be less than human. We would be flesh-covered robots.

PAUL: I don't know about that. The world would be full of wonderful people, thinking noble thoughts. Everybody would love each other. That sounds better than the current system.

KAREN: There is nothing wonderful about choosing love if there is no other option. There is nothing noble about choosing not to kill your neighbor if you are already locked up in prison. Having no free will would be like a prison. Free will is what makes us human. We can make choices. I believe our internal standard of behavior guides us in the choices we make.

PAUL: But people often choose poorly?

KAREN: Far too often.

PAUL: Including you?

KAREN: Most certainly including me.

PAUL: Then what good is your standard? What good is moral law if people don't follow it?

KAREN: What good are speed limits? Don't people ignore them all the time too? Would you say laws are useless because some people disregard them?

PAUL: I guess I would. If nobody pays attention to a law, then it is useless. If people ignore the moral law, then it is useless too.

KAREN: I disagree for two reasons. First, people don't completely disregard moral law. They may break it, but we've already determined they are aware of it. They make excuses for their behavior, or feel shame. So it does have the positive effect of restraining our behavior on some level. Second, the moral law—the ideal—shows us what life could be, and should be. It shows us we need help.

PAUL: I don't think it can be proved either way, but just for the sake of argument; let's assume everybody has an internal sense of moral law. How does that point to the existence of God?

KAREN: I don't see any other explanation for why the moral sense is there. It is not something we would develop or even want, left to ourselves. But since it is there, I have to think somebody put it there.

PAUL: And that would be God?

KAREN: You see right through me, don't you?

PAUL: You are pretty transparent sometimes. Let me offer you a different explanation for your moral law.

KAREN: I can't wait.

PAUL: The moral sense may be a product of evolution.

KAREN: How can that be? How would you call the moral sense an evolutionary improvement?

PAUL: Because it improves the chance for the survival of the group. If people behave morally, and look out for each other, everyone's life improves.

KAREN: I can't argue with that, but I don't see how such behavior comes about by natural selection. I would think selfishness would be sooner rewarded.

PAUL: Look at moral behavior as group selfishness. Then it starts to make sense.

KAREN: It makes no more sense to me than the idea that evolution can produce a sense of irony, or delight in a mountain view. Evolution doesn't do that. God does.

PAUL: You know, this is just the kind of discussion I expected this afternoon. I had a few questions in mind when I got here, but I can't decide if you've answered them, or started me thinking about new ones.

KAREN: It's too early to tell. Besides, it is not a bad thing to look at new ideas once in a while.

PAUL: Don't get too satisfied. I'm not ready to draw any conclusions yet.

KAREN: That's fair enough. For now though, let's at least admit that a secular viewpoint cannot explain the desire for God or a universal moral law. I think that is a good starting point for other discussions.

PAUL: On what topics?

KAREN: Let's consider truth, perhaps, and creation—maybe even the nature of God.

PAUL: I'd better order another latte.

***

Truth As You Like It

PAUL: We might as well get this over with. I can sense that I need to teach you a thing or two about the concept of truth.

KAREN: Go ahead. I am always willing to learn, although I don't always like to be taught.

PAUL: I'll try to be easy on you. I'm sure you like to think truth is something you can believe in, but truth is not carved in granite. It ebbs and flows. Truth is about as constant as my sister's love life.

KAREN: You need to fill in the gaps of that analogy.

PAUL: Every time she gets a crush on some cretin, she believes it is true love. It was fate that brought them together. It will be Romeo and Juliet without the suicide. That is her truth. Then she meets a guy with a flashier car, or a better grasp of NASCAR stats, and the romance turns to ashes. The new guy is really, really her true love. So she has a new truth.

KAREN: I didn't realize you were so disillusioned about love.

PAUL: I'm not. I am suspicious of foolish, romantic notions that change with the weather. I feel the same way about the concept of truth. It's like a paper sack. It just won't hold water.

KAREN: You are very cynical for one so young.

PAUL: Or realistic. Go ahead. Pick any field of human endeavor, and see how truth has changed. Doctors used to think night air was poisonous. That was their truth. Engineers said we would never fly. That was their truth. Coaches thought if a runner broke the four-minute mile, his heart would explode. That was their truth. Now we look at those truths as quaint delusions.

KAREN: You are talking about progressive scientific knowledge. No doubt it changes. When I talk about truth, I mean it in a more universal sense, as in philosophy or religion.

PAUL: You could not have picked worse examples. How many religions have there been throughout the centuries? Thousands. All with their own versions of the truth. And you could fill a library with philosophers trying to define truth. Let's look at one of your favorites. What did Socrates say about truth? He said that all he knew was that he knew nothing.

KAREN: I think he was speaking at the time of knowledge in a more general sense.

PAUL: Maybe he was, and maybe he wasn't. I wasn't there to hear it. But it applies nonetheless. And here is another example that should appeal to you. When Pontius Pilate was about to crucify Jesus, he asked Jesus the famous question, "What is truth?" What was Jesus' response? Silence. Here was a guy who was arguably the greatest philosopher of all time, who had been talking nonstop for three years, and when asked point-blank about the nature of truth, he could not define it. He had no answer.

KAREN: He did not *have* an answer. He *was* the answer. But that is another topic.

PAUL: It's also an evasion. Jesus couldn't define truth because truth can't be defined. It's like a handful of grape jelly. The harder you try to grasp it, the more it squirts out between your fingers.

KAREN: You might have better luck if you use a spoon. But I think searching for truth is more like digging through a box at a garage sale. The deeper you dig, the better chance you have of finding a treasure.

PAUL: Dig all you want. You'll find your treasure, and I'll find mine, and they probably won't be the same. Truth is a relative thing. It's different for everybody.

KAREN: That reminds me of a phrase we heard in high school. I wonder if you remember it. "What is true for you is true for you, and what is true for me is true for me."

PAUL: Mrs. D's class in Family Living. I remember. I thought it was profound.

KAREN: I thought it was nonsense.

PAUL: You don't think people have different opinions about what is true?

KAREN: Of course they do, but opinions and truth are not the same thing. Opinions change. Truth is absolute.

PAUL: Believing in absolute truth is a rather outdated philosophy. All truth is relative to the believer. There is no absolute truth.

KAREN: Let me restate that for you: "It is absolutely true that there is no absolute truth." Do you see the contradiction? You made a statement of objective truth, and denied the existence of truth in the same statement.

PAUL: What do you mean by "objective" truth?

KAREN: Objective truth is true whether anybody knows it or not. It simply is. It is absolute.

PAUL: Let me objectively restate my original thought: "It is true for me that there is no absolute truth." How does that work for you?

KAREN: About as well as Mrs. D's phrase. Let's restate it again: "It is absolutely true that it is true for me that there is no absolute truth." You contradict yourself again.

PAUL: You are just going to keep doing that, aren't you?

KAREN: Mark Twain said there is nothing as irritating as a good example. Are you irritated?

PAUL: No, just stimulated. You seem to be playing word games.

KAREN: As a great writer I know once said: "Words mean things."

PAUL: That's profound.

KAREN: More so than you think. If words have any meaning, then there must be some objective truth in them. Otherwise, they're just random sounds in a meaningless universe.

PAUL: Some of Mrs. D's lectures were like that. Of course there is truth behind words. We obviously have to define words the same way, or we could never communicate, but word definition and overall truth are not the same thing. All I'm saying is that truth means different things to different people.

KAREN: You are confusing truth and opinion again. If we both jump in a swimming pool, you may think the water is too cold, and I may think it's just right, but the temperature of the water remains the same, whatever our opinions may be.

PAUL: Does it matter what the water temperature is? If it's too cold for me, it's too cold for me. If it's just right for you, it's just right for you. We could disagree, but both be telling the truth.

KAREN: We would be telling the truth about our opinions, not about the water temperature. In this case, the temperature is the objective truth. That truth won't change because we have different opinions about it.

PAUL: Water temperature is a fact of nature. Truths about natural laws are different than philosophical truths.

KAREN: How so?

PAUL: We can define natural laws as what always occurs, like water freezing at thirty-two degrees, or apples falling down instead of up. Human truth is harder to define.

KAREN: Why don't you give it a shot?

PAUL: You could say truth is whatever improves us. Whatever makes us better people.

KAREN: That sounds like opinion again. Besides, how do you determine what is better or worse?

PAUL: You are referring to the universal moral code again, aren't you?

KAREN: You can't get away from it.

PAUL: Let's try another definition. Maybe truth is whatever is useful. Whatever leads to desirable behavior. A novel can be true if you learn something from it. Or fairy tales can be true if they teach a moral lesson. It all comes down to what you sincerely believe.

KAREN: So you would define truth as whatever we learn from, or what we sincerely believe?

PAUL: I think we could use that as a working definition.

KAREN: So if you don't learn anything from a statement of truth, or don't believe it, is it no longer true?

PAUL: Give me one of your irritating examples.

KAREN: Let's talk about the Kennedy assassination.

PAUL: Which one?

KAREN: Either would work for my purpose, but let's stick with President Kennedy. I read somewhere that over half of the people in the United States think there was a conspiracy to kill him. They don't believe Lee Harvey Oswald acted alone.

PAUL: I happen to be in that group. I believe the mob had a hand in it to get revenge for Kennedy's attacks on the Teamsters.

KAREN: A lot of people believe that. A lot of people believe Lyndon Johnson had Kennedy killed. Some believe Castro's people did it. I saw a guy on late-night television once who was convinced the CIA did it with a loaded umbrella. The government reports all say that Oswald was the lone assassin.

PAUL: So which one is it?

KAREN: For the purpose of our discussion, it doesn't matter. What matters is that reasonable people sincerely believe completely opposite positions. According to your definition, they are all true. And yet they can't all be true. So your definition must be false.

PAUL: You don't like my definitions of truth. What's yours?

KAREN: Mine is pretty simple. Truth is what *is*, not what you want it to be or what you think it should be. Any other definition is intellectual garbage.

PAUL: You are getting a little worked up over this. Why is the definition of truth as absolute so important to you?

KAREN: Because without absolute truth that can be known on some level, life is pointless. There is no reason to discuss anything. All knowledge is useless, because there is no knowledge.

PAUL: I suppose there is absolute truth in the material world, but not in philosophy or religion.

KAREN: There is no truth in religion?

PAUL: I don't see how you can say there is. There have been thousands of different religions, and all of them claimed a different truth. By your own definition, they were all false.

KAREN: I don't think they were all completely false. Many of them had a great deal of truth in them, or at least pointed toward the truth.

PAUL: Some truth. Partial truth. Pointed toward the truth. Don't talk about absolute truth and then expect to impress me with phrases like that. If you want to know truth, you look for the kind that comes through scientific research. All real knowledge comes through science.

KAREN: How do you know that?

PAUL: Because science is the only real truth. Truth is only true if it can be verified and repeated through experiments.

KAREN: Can you verify that statement with experiments?

PAUL: I suppose not, but I don't have to. I just know it to be true.

KAREN: Do you realize what you are saying? You can't verify that all truth must be verifiable. You claim that truth cannot be assumed, and then assume you know the truth. Who is basing their opinions on faith now?

PAUL: You are trying to ignore the scientific method. You can't do that if you expect to have any credibility as a truth-seeker.

KAREN: I have no problem with the scientific method. It helps prove my case, actually.

PAUL: How is that?

KAREN: Millions of people turn to God and have a positive change in their lives. That sounds repeatable to me.

PAUL: But it is completely subjective. It is all personal feelings and opinions.

KAREN: But it is repeatable. Wasn't that the main point of your scientific method?

PAUL: You can repeat brainwashing and hypnosis too. Does that elevate them to the level of science? Why are you so negative about science anyway? Are you afraid it will prove you wrong?

KAREN: I have no predisposition against science. Science is great at finding out how things happen. It just isn't very good at finding out why. The more important issues of life cannot be judged by science.

PAUL: What issues would those be?

KAREN: The meaning of life for one. The absolute truth of God for another.

PAUL: The dogma of absolute truth is scary. It leads to intolerance, and that is dangerous.

KAREN: Intolerance. That is what everyone is trying to avoid these days, isn't it?

PAUL: Don't tell me you are opposed to tolerance.

KAREN: It depends. What do you mean by tolerance?

PAUL: You are really big on defining terms lately. Socrates tried that, you know, and the Greeks thanked him with a glass of poison.

KAREN: I'll be careful who mixes my drinks. Don't avoid the question. In what sense do you use the word "tolerance"?

PAUL: Tolerance is the recognition that there are no right or wrong opinions. It's actually pretty close to Mrs. D's concept of all truths being equal. How can you say you're right and I'm wrong and still consider yourself tolerant? Tolerance is accepting all points of view as equally valid. It is the most liberating and unifying concept of the last hundred years. I don't think you have quite gotten your mind around it.

KAREN: That's an interesting point of view. And a common one too, I suppose. But I think you confuse your terms. Tolerance should mean accepting the right of others to have different opinions. It does not mean all opinions are equal. I don't find your concept of tolerance liberating or unifying. Just the opposite, in fact.

Your idea of tolerance stifles discussion of ideas and cultures.

PAUL: Stifles ideas? If all ideas are considered valid, then any idea is acceptable. New ideas should be everywhere.

KAREN: I think you have it exactly backward. In your world, no one has the right to pass judgment on any ideas. There is no point in trying to decide what is good or bad or right or wrong, because it is not politically correct to say your answer is any closer to the truth than any other. In your world, no idea is considered superior to another, so why even bother to discuss it?

PAUL: Who are you to say one idea is better than another? Isn't that a little closed-minded?

KAREN: I hope so.

PAUL: You hope you are closed-minded?

KAREN: Of course. Everyone should be, after sifting through the facts. If you are so open-minded that you never reject a bad idea, you're not tolerant, you're immobilized. I'm afraid the concept of tolerance, as you state it, is intellectual laziness masquerading as sophistication. Or maybe it is just cowardice. Whatever it is, it can't be defended without abandoning reason. Sooner or later, any rational person has to make a judgment about something.

PAUL: How can you know whether you are making judgments based on truth or opinion? Maybe the different ideas are not superior or inferior, but just different.

KAREN: I can see how the line between truth and opinion could get blurred, but I suggest to you it is true that some ideas are superior to others.

PAUL: In what way?

KAREN: Some cultures encourage personal freedom; some deny it. Some cultures advocate human rights and dissent; some torture dissenters. They have completely different views on the value of life. Do you mean to tell me you view a culture that tortures its members to be equal with one that doesn't?

PAUL: I try not to make such judgments. There may be considerations that I don't think of, which could cloud my opinion. Besides, once you say "Your ideas are different from mine, so you are inferior," it isn't much of a leap to "Your ideas are different from mine, so I hate you." The feeling of superiority has caused most of the human suffering in history.

KAREN: I said the ideas were inferior, not the person who holds them. I can't believe the philosophy you're trying to defend. This idea of all ideas being equal would have been laughed out of existence any time in human history, except for right now. If everyone had always believed what you do, there would never have been any social progress, because no one could have defined what was an improvement. Do you think there would have been less human suffering if slavery had been considered equal to freedom?

PAUL: I guess you can find isolated examples to illustrate your point, but overall, the idea of cultural superiority is pure arrogance.

KAREN: That's like saying a mathematician is arrogant to claim two plus two equals four. Why can't you choose to believe two plus two equals forty-three?

PAUL: I have a feeling you're going to tell me.

KAREN: This is an easy one. You can't choose the answer you like because truth is not subject to opinion. Not in mathematics and not in life. Truth is not just what you happen to believe. Truth, put simply, is what *is*. And what *is* cannot be equal to what is *not*. Slavery and freedom are not equally valid ideas. Truth and lies are not the same. God either is or is not. Culture, ideas, religion, it doesn't matter. Two facts that contradict each other cannot both be true. That is so obvious to me that I can't conceive of how anyone could not see it.

PAUL: Have you ever heard it said, "The opposite of a great truth is not a lie, but another great truth?"

KAREN: I have heard it. It sounds clever, but I don't know what it means.

PAUL: I don't either, but I thought it might cool you down a little.

KAREN: Oh, I'm cool. But this is important. Before you discuss God, or the meaning of life, or just about anything else, you must accept that there is truth, that truth can be known, and that some ideas simply are not true. Can you live with that?

PAUL: What would Mrs. D think?

KAREN: I'm sure she would be disappointed in me. What do you think?

PAUL: Sometimes I think you win your debates more through persistence than persuasion.

KAREN: My Dad used to tell me, "Patience and perseverance will conquer all." Don't evade the issue. Can we agree on the concept of truth?

PAUL: Once again, I don't feel I should agree with you, but I don't know why, or how to refute you. Let's accept your concept of truth for now. If I come up with something better, I'll let you know.

KAREN: I'll try to be ready.

***

Darwinian Doubts

PAUL: You have been pretty slick so far. I'll give you credit. But the topics have been pretty general. I think it's time to get more specific.

KAREN: You sound like you're going to enjoy this. You must be sure of yourself.

PAUL: I am practically cocky. My case is as solid as an iron rod, driven in frozen ground, encased in concrete. It is an immovable object.

KAREN: Maybe I'll be an irresistible force.

PAUL: Force all you want. You can't win this tug-of-war. The whole scientific world is lined up against you.

KAREN: I didn't even know they were mad at me. What are they so worked up about?

PAUL: Evolution.

KAREN: I had a feeling that was it. Apparently you see Evolution as something I need to refute.

PAUL: If you plan to keep up this quest for God, you had better pay attention to it. You see, Evolution completely disproves Creationism, and eliminates the need for a creator. Darwin killed God.

KAREN: Did he? That is quite an accomplishment for one man.

PAUL: He didn't do it alone. Every scientist in the world is on his side.

KAREN: I don't think it's unanimous. A lot of scientists disagree with Darwin.

PAUL: Then they ignore science to cling to their comforting myths. You are up against it on this one.

KAREN: You think the case for Evolution is airtight?

PAUL: It is not even open to question. If you are going to argue this one, you are beaten before you start.

KAREN: I might surprise you. Let me ask you a question or two. Why do you call Evolution a science, and Creation a myth? Haven't you drawn a conclusion already, just by your definitions? Where is your tolerance?

PAUL: Don't start with me on that. Evolution is proven scientific fact. You can't deny the reality of science just because you want to include God in the discussion. Where is your logic?

KAREN: I think it will surface as we move along. By the way, I didn't try to bring God into the discussion yet. I think that is a little premature. The controversy begins, as I see it, between the theory of Evolution and the theory of Intelligent Design.

PAUL: You are trying to sneak God in the back door. Creationists always do that. You muddy up the waters with your Intelligent Design theories, and then claim to clear up everything with God.

KAREN: You seem to know a lot about my position, considering that you haven't heard it yet.

PAUL: I don't have to hear your position. I know how Creationists think. Or rather, how they don't think. They just repeat the same nonsense often enough that people start to believe it.

KAREN: I see. Once you label me a Creationist, you don't have to listen to me any more. It seems to me you are being closed-minded.

PAUL: You are the one in favor of closed-mindedness, remember?

KAREN: Only after sorting through the facts. Rejecting a bad idea after investigation is a sign of wisdom. Rejecting an idea before it is explored is intellectual snobbery.

PAUL: I don't have to explore the idea of Intelligent Design. We are talking about the physical world here. You said earlier that science has its place. Well, this is it. If you want to determine what happens in the physical, material world, you look at physical, material data. That is science. Science leads to hard truths, the kind you can put your hands on, or view through a microscope. It may lead to truths you don't want to hear, but you can't question science. Not on this.

KAREN: You can't question science? Until fairly recently, scientists thought the world was flat. They thought the best cure for a sick person was to suck their blood out with leeches. Most scientists laughed at Pasteur's theory that germs cause disease. I'm sure those scientists didn't think they should be questioned either.

PAUL: That was all a long time ago. Science has progressed tremendously since those days.

KAREN: No doubt. But I presume you will admit that the scientists of today do make mistakes? They are sometimes wrong?

PAUL: Of course. But the science of Evolution is beyond question.

KAREN: I imagine the doctor reaching into that jar of leeches thought the same thing.

PAUL: I know you have some strange ideas, but you don't seriously doubt the fact of Evolution?

KAREN: Maybe you should tell me what you mean by Evolution.

PAUL: Simple. Species adapt to their surroundings. They change over long periods of time.

KAREN: I think we can agree on that. I have no doubt that species change over time.

PAUL: Then what is the problem?

KAREN: There is none, as far as your definition goes. But I wonder if you don't mean more than you say.

PAUL: I don't follow you.

KAREN: Let's broaden your definition of Evolution a bit and see where that takes us. As I understand it, the theory of Evolution states that life began at the cellular level from inanimate, lifeless matter. The cells evolved into more and more complex organisms, and over millions of years, through natural selection and mutation, all vegetation and animal life evolved from these organisms. How does that sound?

PAUL: I think you put that very well. You have a gift for being succinct.

KAREN: Thank you. We will see if you think so in a few minutes. Did I reasonably state your definition of Evolution?

PAUL: Not just mine. Pretty much every biology professor or scientist would define it the same way.

KAREN: They would define it that way, but I wonder how many have examined the evidence to see if it makes sense. I wonder how many just accept the theory as proven fact.

PAUL: You aren't a scientist. How can you presume to challenge professionals in their field of expertise?

KAREN: I'm not a mathematics professor either, but I understand algebra and geometry. I know enough about research methods to tell when Evolutionists twist the facts to fit their theory instead of their theory to fit the facts.

PAUL: I know where this is going. You are going to suggest Intelligent Design as an alternative to Evolution. Then you are going to assume an Intelligent Designer. Then you are going to call the Designer God.

KAREN: Let's take this a step at a time. For the moment, I just want to see if Evolution is a workable theory.

PAUL: But there is no reasonable scientific alternative to Evolution. You have to accept it. What else is there?

KAREN: There may be something else, and there may not. Even if there is not, I refuse to accept a doubtful theory just because I can't think of a better one. With your respect for scientific methods, I would expect you to feel the same way.

PAUL: I do feel the same way, but the theory of Evolution is not doubtful. It is proven science.

KAREN: Or maybe it's just been repeated enough that people believe it. Let's look at the facts for a moment, and see where they lead us.

PAUL: Fire away.

KAREN: Would you say the main component of Darwin's theory of Evolution is natural selection? In other words, the members of a species best suited to their environment will reproduce. Adaptations will occur purely by chance or accident, but they lead to survival of the fittest. Is that right?

PAUL: I would say that is the main component of Darwin's theory, and there is plenty of evidence for it.

KAREN: For example?

58

PAUL: Look around a zoo. Giraffes have long necks to eat leaves out of tree tops. Anteaters have long noses to eat ants out of anthills. Gazelles are fast enough to outrun lions, who have teeth and claws to tear at gazelle flesh. Penguins stay warm on ice. Fish breathe underwater. It is amazing, really, to think of how well adapted animals are to their environments. That seems ample proof of Evolution to me.

KAREN: It seems ample proof that animals are well suited to their environments. I don't see how it proves they all started at the same point and changed through Evolution. That is a gigantic leap of faith.

PAUL: I prefer not to use the word faith in relation to science. I base my opinions on evidence.

KAREN: Your evidence shows that different animals have different abilities. A giraffe is nothing like an anteater, or a lion like a gazelle. Why do you conclude they all descended from a common ancestor?

PAUL: Because a giraffe is very much like an anteater, and a lion and a gazelle. They all have stomachs, hearts, lungs. They all have eyes and ears and noses and tails. Nervous systems, brains, legs, hair, bones. The differences are slight modifications to adapt to environment.

KAREN: That is a good point, but it occurs to me that a Ford is very similar to a Toyota, or a Rolls Royce.

Does that mean they were all made in the same factory?

PAUL: I think I can use your example against you.

KAREN: Jump right in.

PAUL: The vehicles you mentioned are similar because they all descended from the same original automobile. They were adapted over time to meet the needs of their users. It is vehicular Evolution.

KAREN: I admire the way your mind works.

PAUL: So you see the logic?

KAREN: I don't think logic is the word I would use. Your example has a fatal flaw.

PAUL: Enlighten me. What is the fatal flaw?

KAREN: Vehicles are designed. The adaptations were designed. If you could show me where a car had randomly assembled itself in a junkyard, I might be convinced. Or if it grew aerodynamic fenders and leather seats. I like leather seats.

PAUL: I thought you were a fan of crushed red velvet, or fake leopard skin.

KAREN: That was just a phase. My tastes have evolved.

PAUL: Let's hope so. Anyway, let me see if I can give you a better example of Evolution.

KAREN: Please do.

PAUL: Greyhounds.

KAREN: The dogs or the buses?

PAUL: The dogs. By mating only the leanest, fastest animals, breeders have developed dogs that are built to run. It is the same thing with cattle. Breeders produce the healthiest cattle with the fastest growth by careful selection and breeding. The artificial selection by breeders simulates natural selection in the wild.

KAREN: Does it? You claim that a random natural process can produce beneficial modifications in an animal, and then give an example of modification by Design. Which theory are you trying to prove?

PAUL: Natural selection takes an incredible length of time. Artificial selection simply speeds up the process.

KAREN: I don't think it is that simple. By selecting artificially, you inject human intelligence into the mix. Your selection is no longer random, but purposeful.

PAUL: Can you think of a better way to simulate random selection?

KAREN: No. Unfortunately, neither can anyone else. Any test you design cannot, by definition, be completely random if it is designed by an intelligent agent. Your theory of Evolution cannot be verified by the scientific method in which you place so much faith.

PAUL: I wish you would stop using that word. I do not accept Evolution on faith. I deduce it from the evidence.

KAREN: So Evolution is now a deduction? I thought it was proven scientific fact.

PAUL: Evolution is adaptation, and adaptation is proven fact. Insects grow resistant to insecticides every few years, so the chemicals have to be modified. Bacteria become immune to anti-bacterial agents. Let's make it something easier to see. Lions eat slow gazelles. Fast gazelles run away to produce more fast gazelles. Short giraffes starve to death. Tall giraffes produce more tall giraffes. Slow or stupid animals die young. Nature is harsh. Only the fittest survive to reproduce. This is simply a fact of nature. You can't deny it.

KAREN: I don't deny that natural selection exists, or that it helps maintain a species. I have no doubt that giraffes and gazelles and lions adapt to their surroundings. So do insects and bacteria, as creepy as that is.

PAUL: Then where is the disagreement?

KAREN: The disagreement is over where the theory goes next. If Evolution were defined only as change within a species, I would have no problem with it. But the theory of Evolution goes beyond that. It claims the mechanism of natural selection can change one species into another. It claims that gazelles and lions and giraffes all descended from the same source. That's an assumption as big as the Grand Canyon, with no solid evidence to support it. Just because they're similar doesn't mean they're related.

PAUL: Then how do you explain the similarity?

KAREN: For the moment, I don't have to explain it. We are examining the possibility of Evolution now, and whether it explains the similarities. I don't think it does, and we are back to the point where you accept Evolution not because there is reasonable evidence for it, but because you don't want to consider anything else.

PAUL: There is definitely evidence for adaptation within a species. Would you agree?

KAREN: Certainly.

PAUL: Then it seems only reasonable to deduce that, given enough time, adaptation to different environments would lead to different species. The similarity between species only helps lead to that very reasonable conclusion.

KAREN: I don't see any facts that would lead me to that conclusion. Only assumptions. If new species could be created through natural selection, then why can't artificial selection do the same thing? Why haven't breeders developed new species? They can breed greyhounds, but they can't turn them into some kind of mutated monster. Perhaps that is because genetics won't allow a dog to turn into anything but a variation of a dog. Not through natural or artificial selection.

PAUL: We could argue this all day without reaching a conclusion. Let me ask you a question that may settle this. What would it take to overcome your objections? What one piece of evidence would convince you that Evolution is true?

KAREN: I don't know if there is one piece of evidence that would convince me, but there is one piece you really need. Even Darwin admitted the lack of this evidence would seriously compromise his theory.

PAUL: Let me have it. What do I need to produce?

KAREN: Consider this. If you believe all animals descended from the same source, and they varied through chance and mutation over millions of years to develop into all the different species we now see; if you believe human beings began as ape-like creatures, and developed over millions of years into the attractive, coffee drinking individuals at this table, then there should be museums on every corner full of bones and fossils proving those very facts. There should be thousands of half-ape, half-human skeletons preserved in ancient mud somewhere. There should be millions of fossils available to show us how all of those species changed from one to another.

PAUL: I thought you had a gift for being succinct.

KAREN: My apologies. Let's just say I call your attention to the curious fact of the fossil record.

PAUL: But there is no such fossil record.

KAREN: That is the curious fact.

***

Signs of Design

PAUL: It may be surprising that the fossil record of Evolution is so limited, but that doesn't prove no evolving life forms ever existed. Absence of evidence is not evidence of absence.

KAREN: I wish I had said that.

PAUL: Feel free to use it sometime.

KAREN: Perhaps in another context. You have to admit the lack of fossil evidence casts doubt on the theory of Evolution, as Darwin himself said it would.

PAUL: How so?

KAREN: If millions of evolving life forms existed over millions of years, where are their remains? Why do we only find the remains of animals in their completed states?

PAUL: We hadn't even found those until fairly recently. Maybe the others just haven't been found yet.

KAREN: So you accept the theory of Evolution based on evidence that doesn't exist, in the hope that it will? Your faith is impressive.

PAUL: I do not have faith. I have a scientific position. You don't.

KAREN: I don't? You claim that random chance can explain the existence of life, and I say it can't. It seems to me we just have opposing theories. Yet you say yours is scientific and mine is not. Why is that?

PAUL: Because your theory includes an Intelligent Designer. The idea of a creator is religious, not scientific.

KAREN: It seems to me you have arbitrarily applied a "religious" label to the Intelligent Design theory, just so you can ignore the evidence.

PAUL: The label is not arbitrary, it is accurate. Intelligent Design is a religious theory, and it does not belong in a scientific discussion, and it certainly does not belong in a biology class, which some of your fellow believers would like to see.

KAREN: It belongs in a biology class if evidence points toward Intelligent Design.

PAUL: I don't know how much I trust your opinion about a biology class. I never saw anybody as bored with biology as you were.

KAREN: I can't say I enjoyed identifying the internal parts of a dissected piglet.

PAUL: I liked cutting up the worms.

KAREN: Typical high school boy.

PAUL: I was crude, maybe, but harmless. And I don't remember hearing anything about Intelligent Design from Mr. Snodgrass. Which was a good thing. There is no good evidence for it, and it shouldn't be discussed in school.

KAREN: You can't reject evidence because it doesn't fit your preconceived notions. And I thought school was where different ideas were supposed to be debated, not banned from discussion.

PAUL: The first amendment to the Constitution bans discussing religion in the schools.

KAREN: The first amendment says Congress shall pass no law prohibiting the free exercise of religion. I don't see how that means you can't discuss religion in schools.

PAUL: I believe the amendment also says the government shall not establish a religion. That's why it has to stay out of the schools. Because if it is taught in state schools, it implies endorsement by the state. That seems pretty obvious to me.

KAREN: Schools teach about terrorists too. That doesn't mean they endorse their activities. Look, I'm not saying schools should conduct Bible studies, but you can't just call Intelligent Design religious dogma, and ban all discussion. If there is a scientific disagreement about Evolution versus Intelligent Design, students have a right to hear the evidence.

PAUL: But the evidence for Intelligent Design cannot be taken seriously. It cannot be proven through experiments and observation.

KAREN: I'm afraid Evolution cannot be proven through experiments and observation either. It can be deduced, or assumed, or even violently defended, but it cannot be proven. Believing in either theory requires a certain amount of faith.

PAUL: All right. We both have faith in our theories. In order to support one or the other, you have to go by the weight of the evidence, and that is on my side.

KAREN: You know I'm going to disagree with that, don't you?

PAUL: As sure as the turning of the earth.

KAREN: It is good to have something in life you can be sure of.

PAUL: True, but you'd think that by now I could come up with something other than you.

KAREN: Maybe we can find you something.

PAUL: Like a creator?

KAREN: Possibly. Maybe even more than that.

PAUL: Don't get ahead of yourself. You haven't given me any evidence for a creator yet.

KAREN: Let me give you some. Darwinists and atheists usually teach that the universe has always existed, and always will. It had no beginning, and no end, so no creator is required. As Carl Sagan said, the universe is "all that is, or ever was, or ever will be."

PAUL: I guess I can live with that.

KAREN: Not unless you cling to your comforting myths. Most scientists now believe the universe began at a certain point in time. A creation point, you might say. They call it the Big Bang.

PAUL: I'm familiar with the theory. How does the Big Bang point to a creator?

KAREN: How else do you explain it? Something caused the universe to explode into being at a particular point in time.

PAUL: Some*thing* did, I suppose, like gravity or magnetism or thermodynamic forces. The cause was not necessarily a some*body*.

KAREN: That is what we are trying to determine. I submit that nothing happens without a cause. Including creation. Logic tells us there must be a creator, a Designer.

PAUL: Then who created the creator? If nothing happens without a cause, what caused your Designer to spring into existence?

KAREN: Maybe I didn't phrase that correctly. I should have said that anything that has been created has a cause. Since God has always existed, he does not require a cause. He is the ultimate cause.

PAUL: So logic tells you that everything has a cause except for the one thing whose existence you are trying to prove. You've twisted your logic into a philosophical pretzel. I think I can pretty much discount that. Maybe you should try to give me some science.

KAREN: All right. How about all the information stored in your DNA?

PAUL: I'm a big fan of DNA, but I don't see how it helps your Intelligent Design theory. Every DNA cell in our bodies contains more information than an encyclopedia. It determines our size, shape, eye color—probably how smart we are. It is pretty amazing stuff, that DNA, and it came about through Evolution. Who needs a creator when you have DNA?

KAREN: It is hard for me to believe that much information developed by random chance. If you find an encyclopedia lying on a beach, do you assume it developed itself? Or was it designed?

PAUL: Encyclopedias are not alive. They cannot evolve. Human cells can.

KAREN: Human cells can change, I suppose. But you assume that cells can improve themselves, or create information where there is none. There is no evidence to support either theory. Evolutionists just assume they must be true.

PAUL: It seems like a logical assumption.

KAREN: It seems no more logical to me than assuming my computer wrote its own operating code. Complex information cannot develop itself. It must be the product of an Intelligent Designer.

PAUL: If life can come about from inanimate matter, it can certainly create information.

KAREN: That is a pretty big "if".

PAUL: I'll give you something to make that "if" a lot smaller. I know you have heard of the experiment by Stanley Miller in the 1950's. It showed that proteins could develop in the atmosphere that was present on earth billions of years ago. If proteins develop, then life could come from there. Miller proved life could develop spontaneously. That is the beginning of Evolution.

KAREN: I'm glad you brought that up. If you dig a little deeper, you will find that the atmosphere Miller used in his experiment did not reflect the atmosphere on earth at the time he proposed. If the correct atmosphere is reproduced, life has no chance to develop. The conclusions originally drawn from Miller's experiment are no longer considered valid.

PAUL: If that is true, then why was the experiment cited in my old textbook?

KAREN: What reasons occur to you?

PAUL: Maybe you are wrong. Or maybe it was just an honest mistake.

KAREN: I'm not wrong. Feel free to investigate it yourself. And if Evolutionists make a mistake on something this basic, how can you trust the rest of their evidence?

PAUL: Haven't you ever made a mistake?

KAREN: Lots of them. I'll probably make a lot more. But the truth about the Miller experiment has been known for years, yet many Evolutionists still cite it as evidence to support their theory of spontaneous life.

PAUL: I'll bet you have an opinion about why they do that.

KAREN: I am willing to listen to another explanation, but I only see two possibilities. Either Evolutionists are willing to falsify the data to support their theory, or they haven't done enough research to know the truth. Neither is a very flattering picture.

PAUL: I don't think it is productive to attack scientists and teachers.

KAREN: That reminds me of President Harry Truman. He was accused of giving his opponents Hell. He said, "I don't give them Hell. I just tell the truth on them, and they think it's Hell."

PAUL: Harry Truman was about as stubborn as you are. Let's drop the Miller experiment, and get back to DNA. Why couldn't the information in DNA develop at random? Why couldn't information that improved the cell develop at the cellular level?

KAREN: First of all, I would tell you that it has never been observed. Secondly, it flies against all common sense. In no other instance can you show me organized information without intelligence. Nowhere.

PAUL: It may not have been observed, but that doesn't mean it isn't true. It is the only logical explanation for all the information present in DNA.

KAREN: It is the only explanation Evolutionary theory will allow. That doesn't mean it is logical. You are forced to believe organized information can come from chaos, or your whole system falls apart. I think it is more logical to believe that information came from intelligence, which means an Intelligent Designer.

PAUL: Once again, I don't see conclusive evidence, only deductions.

KAREN: Here is another deduction we can make. There must be intelligence behind creation, because we think there must be.

PAUL: You are talking in circles.

KAREN: Not really. "I think, therefore I am." Get it?

PAUL: No. What is your point?

KAREN: Humans are self-reflecting animals. We can think, and not only that, we can reflect on the fact that we can think. I am talking about consciousness. How can inanimate matter evolve into reflective, intelligent creatures unless there is intelligence behind the creation of the creatures?

PAUL: I am amazed that you can get thoughts like that from your mind to your mouth.

KAREN: I was well designed.

PAUL: Or conveniently evolved. Your point about self-reflection is a good one, but it is still a deduction based on philosophy rather than science.

KAREN: Let me try another example. Have you heard of irreducible complexity?

PAUL: I have. That is the idea that Evolution is an impossible explanation for some organisms because they couldn't function if they were not complete in their present form. No intermediate steps could have worked, or possibly even survived.

KAREN: Well put. Scientists and biologists—who are much smarter than I am—have illustrated that irreducible complexity exists at the cellular level. In other words, the inner workings of cells are so complex that they could not have developed step by step. Take away any piece, and the cell is useless. It is fascinating research, and it certainly points towards Design rather than Evolution, but it is a little over my head. I prefer a simpler example.

PAUL: And that would be?

KAREN: The eyeball.

PAUL: It is irreducibly complex?

KAREN: Which part of it could you remove and still be able to see? It fits the theory perfectly. The eye would not have been a beneficial change unless it was complete, so it could not have evolved over time through small modifications. Yet here it is, in all its complexity, complete and functioning. It must have come into being all at once. By Design.

PAUL: Or mutation. Genetic mutation could explain drastic changes in an organism. In fact, it could explain why we don't see fossils of animals undergoing changes. Maybe they mutated overnight.

KAREN: When have you ever seen a mutation that was beneficial instead of harmful? And how does an organ as complex as the human eye suddenly mutate from nothing to something? And why did all of these mutations in all these species happen at the same time? If this is your position, then you have abandoned what you called the main component of Evolutionary theory. Descent through gradual modification disappears.

PAUL: I'm trying to twist the theory to fit the facts.

KAREN: I'm glad to hear it, but the facts are going to be pretty tough on you. They all point towards Design.

PAUL: They do the way you present them.

KAREN: I hope I present them honestly and without prejudice. I didn't start out believing in Intelligent Design, you know. I accepted the theory of Evolution for a long time. But as I investigated the concept, I found the theory that made more sense on any level was Intelligent Design. I didn't especially want to believe it, but I could not honestly look at the evidence and reach any other conclusion.

PAUL: So now you are hostile towards Evolutionists?

KAREN: Hardly. I almost feel sorry for Evolutionists. They are forced to believe in some pretty bizarre stuff.

PAUL: More bizarre than a grey-bearded old man on a white throne speaking the universe into existence?

KAREN: I don't remember saying anything about beards or thrones. I base my beliefs on the evidence as it now stands. I believe it points to an Intelligent Designer. In order to believe in Evolution, you have to believe the unbelievable.

PAUL: Such as?

KAREN: You must believe that life began from nothing; that organized information and intelligence developed from chaos; that random chance can improve and fine-tune organisms; that inanimate matter can develop into beings capable of self-reflection; and that organisms so complex they cannot function with any missing parts evolved one piece at a time.

PAUL: I never looked at it that way.

KAREN: You were never taught to look at it that way. Neither was I. I tried for a long time to believe these things, but I finally had to give up. Like I said earlier, it takes faith to believe in Evolution. I'm afraid the most ardent believers choose that faith over the evidence for Intelligent Design simply because they don't want to believe in a Designer.

PAUL: You are beginning to shake my confidence.

KAREN: That's what friends are for.

***

The Long and Winding Road

PAUL: Some friend you are. I was perfectly comfortable with my views until you started in on me. Now I know as much as I ever did, I just don't know if any of it is true.

KAREN: That is the beginning of understanding.

PAUL: Or insanity.

KAREN: Sometimes it's hard to tell the two apart. A fool thinks himself wise, and a wise man knows himself to be a fool. At least you will now consider that there might be a creator, a god of some kind, right?

PAUL: I guess I always suspected there was a god of some kind. A universal spirit. The spirit of "good" that is out there.

KAREN: A spirit of "good"? Is that your definition of God?

PAUL: It will do. Any religion will tell you there is a spirit that envelops the whole world, but it isn't necessarily the Jewish or Christian God, it's just a universal spirit you can tap into. We're all part of that spirit, and it's in all of us. It doesn't matter what road you take to get to it, as long as you get in touch with your inner self. Someone once said, "The finding of God is coming to one's self."

KAREN: Whoever said that got it backwards. The finding of God should be losing one's self. Frankly, I'm not all that interested in getting in touch with my inner self. I'm more concerned with getting in touch with God and having a relationship with him.

PAUL: We obviously view our holy spirits differently. Mine is universal. It is everywhere. It is too large to have a relationship with.

KAREN: Or too small. My God is everywhere, but can also be intimate. He is not so limited that he can't have a relationship with me on a personal level.

PAUL: I guess it's the personal part of it that I don't get. How can you have a personal relationship with a universal spirit? How do you talk to consciousness? How do you pray to a feeling?

KAREN: Well, you can't. Just like a vague spirit couldn't design the world, and inject it with intelligence. But a personal God could. A God who can communicate—who can be known.

PAUL: You mean known on a personal level? Like you and I know each other?

KAREN: That's what I mean. Listen. If God is personal, and wants us to develop a relationship with him, how do you think he would communicate that to us?

PAUL: I suspect you think he would become a man.

KAREN: I'm being transparent again, aren't I?

PAUL: You can't help yourself. Seriously though, a person is either God or man. You can't be both.

KAREN: Why not? If God were trying to communicate with humans, what would be a better way to do it?

PAUL: Look, I don't know. I'm not God. I don't know the best way for him to communicate with humans. But I'm pretty sure that a man can't turn into God.

KAREN: I'm pretty sure of that too. Man can't turn into God. But don't you think God could turn into man?

PAUL: He probably could, but why would he? Why would he degrade himself by becoming a dirty, hungry animal, with sore feet and calluses and mosquito bites?

KAREN: Maybe because the people he wanted to communicate with were dirty, hungry animals with sore feet and calluses. I don't know how he justified the mosquito bites. I'm opposed to them, personally.

PAUL: I'm not all that fond of calluses either. If you were God, wouldn't you find an easier way to get your message across?

KAREN: I'm not sure an easier way would have been as effective. After all, if you want a potato, you plant a potato. If you want to teach a man, it's convenient to be a man.

PAUL: Convenient maybe, but not necessarily credible. There have always been crazies around who claimed to be God. If God turned into a man, what makes you think anybody would listen to him? Why wouldn't they just think he was a nut?

KAREN: A lot of them would. But don't you wonder what he would say when he got here?

PAUL: I suspect he would have a lot to say. Maybe he would finally tell you the meaning of life, so you could lighten up a little. He would probably have a pretty good list of rules to live by. It wouldn't be worth the trouble of coming otherwise.

KAREN: True enough. How do you think people would react to being told how to live?

PAUL: How do you think? Most of them would be really ticked off.

KAREN: Why is that?

PAUL: Think about it. If he was really God, he'd point out how rotten most human behavior is.

KAREN: You don't think people would find that instructive?

PAUL: I think they would find it irritating. People don't like to be told they are less than perfect. It attacks their self-esteem.

KAREN: Only if they're insecure.

PAUL: Which includes anybody I ever met, except you. What about those TV preachers that beg for money and promise prosperity? This man/god of yours would surely tell them they were hypocrites and liars. How do you think they would like that?

KAREN: Probably not so much.

PAUL: Of course not. The problem is, no matter how good his message was, most people wouldn't like what he said, or even believe he was God. Most of the pious preachers would sic the dog on him. They would ruin him if they could, just to protect themselves.

KAREN: It can be dangerous to upset the social order.

PAUL: Not just *can* be. It *is* dangerous. Anybody that upsets the status quo is in danger. It's like we said about Socrates. He disagreed with the ruling powers in Athens, and they killed him for it.

KAREN: He was sacrificed in the name of truth?

PAUL: It depends on who you ask. His followers certainly thought so.

KAREN: So do I. Socrates' fate shows what can happen to a man who confronts the established system of ideas. And I think it's a pretty good bet that if God came to earth in human form, he would do just that.

PAUL: That's why he would need to choose the right spot to appear. It would have to be somewhere that was extremely tolerant of different ideas.

KAREN: I don't think so. If the tolerance you describe is the equality of all ideas, then why would his ideas matter any more than yours or mine? Why would anyone listen, or even care? I think he would have to enter human history in a place where the idea of God was very well defined, so there would be no doubt about his claim.

PAUL: I don't know. It seems to me he would want to appear somewhere where God could be just about anything, or anybody, so the people would be open to the idea.

KAREN: I have to disagree again. If God can be anything, than anything can be God. If God appeared in a place with a philosophy like that, he would have no more impact than a midnight infomercial. That kind of tolerance doesn't reveal truth, it obscures it.

PAUL: Tolerant or not, he would have the most impact in the modern world.

KAREN: Why is that?

PAUL: Mass communication. He could get his message out to everybody at the same time. Over cable news, or talk shows.

KAREN: It is hard for me to imagine God on a talk show, squeezed in between a bubbly young starlet and a juggler from Omaha.

PAUL: I think God would get top billing.

KAREN: Probably, but I don't think modern America would be the right place. Its idea of God is too fuzzy.

PAUL: I don't see what you mean.

KAREN: You alluded to it earlier. People think they can take any path to God. American culture has adopted pieces of Buddhism, Hinduism, paganism, and about any other "ism" you can think of. If God can be anything you like, then one more guy shouting in the wilderness wouldn't be a big deal.

PAUL: So the best place for God to appear is not modern America. That leaves about an infinite number of other times and places.

KAREN: Not really. I think God would want to appear where he had already prepared the people. Someplace where they knew him, somewhere he was expected, and where they would understand the magnitude of his claim to be God.

PAUL: You sound like you have somewhere in mind.

KAREN: I try never to lead up to a conclusion if I don't have one.

PAUL: Your conclusion is obvious. You think God stepped into human history in Judea, two thousand years ago. Born in Bethlehem, raised in Nazareth, and crucified in Jerusalem.

KAREN: Jesus of Nazareth. Born, raised, and crucified as a Jew. It's important to remember that.

PAUL: Of course he was a Jew. How could he not have been? He was raised in a Jewish home and lived in a Jewish culture. Why is that so important?

KAREN: Because it makes his claim to be God so outrageous, and so understandable. If he had made that claim in a pagan society, it would have been almost meaningless, because pagans believed God was everything and everything was God. Jews were nearly alone in their belief that there was one God, that he created the universe, and that he was outside the world. They respected him so deeply they would not even speak his name. So when Jesus claimed to be the great "I AM," they knew exactly what he meant.

PAUL: But Jesus never said he was God. He said God was within us. He taught and philosophized and healed and transformed lives. But he never said he was God. He never made that claim.

KAREN: So if a man shows up at your house in a van that has "Electricians Are Us" printed on the side, and repairs a circuit breaker in your house, and wires your garage for power, do you deny his profession because he never said the exact words "I am an electrician"?

PAUL: Take a breath, now. You're not going to tell me Jesus wired garages too, are you?

KAREN: I doubt he would have had the time. But he did give evidence that he was God.

PAUL: What kind of evidence can you give that you are God?

KAREN: He allowed people to worship him as God. He forgave sins. Not sins against him, but sins against others. Who can do that, other than God?

PAUL: I knew a guy once who did that. He lived in a box.

KAREN: I'm not surprised. If a person claims to be God, there are only two possibilities. He either is God or is not. If he is not, then he's either crazy or exceedingly evil. No one who knew or has studied Jesus found him to be either. What does that tell you?

PAUL: It tells me you are trying to make your conclusion sound logical, whether it is or not. But Jesus never actually claimed to be God, did he?

KAREN: He told the lady at the well that he was the Messiah. He told the Pharisees that "before Abraham was, I AM." The Jews had no trouble understanding his meaning, because there was no other way they could interpret that statement. In the context in which he spoke, his meaning was unmistakable. Jesus claimed to be God. Some of the Jews believed him. Some didn't. You have to decide what you believe.

PAUL: I believe it is very possible, even likely, that Jesus was the greatest teacher who ever lived, but not God.

KAREN: What made him the greatest teacher who ever lived?

PAUL: He taught such great truths. You know, "Love your neighbor," and all that.

KAREN: Most of what he said had been taught before. Be good to your neighbor. Don't always put yourself first. Believe in something bigger than yourself. Philosophers have been saying those things since the beginning of time. If he was not God, why should his words carry any more weight than Plato, or Confucius, or the Renaissance philosophers?

PAUL: You are finally coming around to my way of thinking. They all say the same thing, so it doesn't matter which one you follow.

KAREN: Parts of their philosophies were similar, but if one of them was God, he is the one to follow. If Jesus was not God, then Christianity is no more important than any other philosophy or religion. They are all man-made devices. You can throw them all in the trash if you like. Or believe them if you like. It doesn't matter. But if Jesus was who he said he was, then it matters a great deal who you listen to. Following Jesus is walking down the road to God.

PAUL: I'm starting to think you disagree with me just so you can prove me wrong. You take a perverse pleasure in that, don't you?

KAREN: I'm not trying to impress anybody with my debating skills. I'm just a beggar trying to tell another beggar where to find food.

PAUL: And the beggar won't listen?

KAREN: The beggar seems to be trying very hard not to believe there is a feast around the corner.

PAUL: Maybe the beggar isn't hungry.

KAREN: You remind me of the trip I took to Alaska last summer.

PAUL: You saw beggars in Anchorage?

KAREN: No. I saw moose. But not as many as I should have.

PAUL: How come?

KAREN: The snow was so deep the winter before that the moose couldn't find food, so they wandered out of the woods to find something to eat. The folks in Anchorage took pity on them, and broke open bales of hay around the timber's edge. The moose gobbled it up like you do fried chicken.

PAUL: Fried chicken is one of life's great pleasures. It might even be evidence for an Intelligent Designer.

KAREN: I never thought to bring that up.

PAUL: You missed your chance. Now I want to see how you tie in a hay-eating moose with Jesus.

KAREN: I'm not sure you are going to like this.

PAUL: I'll take a chance. What happened?

KAREN: The moose died. They walked home with full bellies and contented moose smiles, but the problem was that moose stomachs are not designed to digest hay. They starved to death with their bellies full.

PAUL: And how does that apply to me?

KAREN: The moose were content because their bellies were full of comforting food they couldn't use. You are content because your mind is full of comforting ideas you can't defend.

PAUL: That is rather insulting.

KAREN: It was not meant as an insult, just an observation.

PAUL: I'll try to take it that way. Look, Jesus may be a path to God—whatever that is, but I believe there are many ways to reach God. What makes you think Jesus is the only way? What makes you think he was who he said he was?

KAREN: You have asked the most important question of the last two thousand years. "Was Jesus who he said he was?" Libraries have been written trying to answer that single question.

PAUL: And you think we can decide it here over a cup of coffee?

KAREN: I think I can answer that question in twenty minutes.

PAUL: I'll start the clock.

***

Pomp and Circumstance

PAUL: If Jesus claimed to be God, he must not have been very convincing. Two-thirds of the people in the world don't believe it.

KAREN: How did you come up with that figure?

PAUL: Just look at the people who don't believe. Atheists think Jesus was a psycho, or worse. Muslims say he was a prophet. Jews say he was an insightful Rabbi. Why should I believe he was more than that?

KAREN: Millions of people do. Doesn't that persuade you?

PAUL: Millions don't. Does that persuade you?

KAREN: Good point. Let's talk about you for a minute. You do believe that Jesus lived, right? I mean that he was an actual historical figure?

PAUL: I believe he lived as a man, sure. Even atheists believe that.

94

KAREN: I just want to be clear on that before we go any farther. Some people believe that Jesus himself was a myth. If we are past that nonsense, you need to read the accounts of Jesus' life and ministry. Base your conclusion on the picture presented there.

PAUL: What do you mean, the picture presented there?

KAREN: The picture of Jesus. What was he like? What did he say? What did he do? Are any of his actions contrary to what you would expect from God?

PAUL: In other words—was he crazy? Was he a liar?

KAREN: Those are the two obvious questions. Blunt, but obvious.

PAUL: Here is another one that may not be so obvious: Was he successful?

KAREN: Successful in what way?

PAUL: In accomplishing anything. It seems unlikely to me that Jesus was God, because his mission failed. The kind of god you describe would not fail.

KAREN: You lost me. How did he fail?

PAUL: Nothing changed because he was here. If God became human to change how we live, he sure drew a flat blank zero. It's like the French philosopher Voltaire said, "Men have always been liars, cheats, thieves, gluttons, drunkards, hypocrites and fools."

KAREN: That is probably an incomplete list.

PAUL: No doubt. But it will do to show how little difference Jesus made in the world.

KAREN: I'm surprised at you. I thought it was part of your New Age philosophy to believe that all humans are basically good.

PAUL: It is, but it's pretty hard to hold that theory if you study history, or even watch the evening news.

KAREN: I agree completely. Do you realize that you have just stated a basic piece of Christian doctrine?

PAUL: Not on purpose.

KAREN: Probably not, but it's there, just the same. We're all sinners. We all fall short of the standard of God, which means we all need a Savior. Guess who that is?

PAUL: You never miss a chance, do you?

KAREN: I try to be ready.

PAUL: Be ready for this: If Jesus was our Savior, then why didn't we change as a result of his being here? Why do we treat each other as badly as we did before he came? Doesn't that show that his mission failed?

KAREN: It depends on how you define the mission. I don't think God became human and died on the cross to make us nice to one another. Jesus came to save our souls. And He does that one person at a time, in a very personal manner. His mission, if you choose to state it that way, was a success—and is a success, because it continues even now.

PAUL: It is an odd kind of success. The history of the human race is written in blood. Before and after Jesus. His appearance hasn't made any difference to most of the people in the world. If he was God, how could he be such a dismal failure?

KAREN: I don't think you can judge the success of Jesus' mission by those who ignored his message. You have to look at those who accepted it. They have made a difference in the world. One person at a time. Besides, God knew most people would reject him and his message of redemption. It is a wide path that leads away from God, and many take it.

PAUL: Many take it, that's for sure. Doesn't that show that Jesus was a poor salesman? He offers the deal of a lifetime, and most people slam the door in his face. Would so many people ignore him if he was God?

KAREN: This goes back to our discussion of free will. Jesus stands at the door and knocks. We get to choose whether we open the door. Jesus is not made irrelevant because so many make the wrong choice. Truth doesn't change because people choose not to believe it.

PAUL: I think we have been over that ground already. Maybe I'll have better luck with one of the obvious questions. How do you know Jesus wasn't just crazy?

KAREN: Crazy people act crazy. Jesus didn't.

PAUL: It could be that you are crazy. Then you wouldn't know the difference.

KAREN: I guess that's true. I might be completely out of my mind. That doesn't say much for your taste in coffee companions, does it?

PAUL: Maybe I'm crazy too.

KAREN: Sometimes I think we both are, but Jesus wasn't.

PAUL: He was crazy if he believed he was God.

KAREN: Not if he was God. Since that's what we're trying to determine, you can't use that as a criteria to judge his sanity.

PAUL: Then what can you use?

KAREN: Several things. A sane man would maintain long-term relationships with a variety of people. Jesus did that. A sane man would keep his emotions under control even when things didn't go his way. Jesus did that. He had a firm grasp of reality. He had insight into human nature like no one before or since. If you add it all up, that looks like a sound mind to me.

PAUL: He kept his emotions under control? I thought he broke down at Lazarus' funeral. He cried like a little girl.

KAREN: He wept, if that's what you mean. Lazarus was his friend. I don't think it's a sign of mental illness to cry when a friend dies.

PAUL: Why would he cry if he knew he was going to raise Lazarus from the dead? That seems unstable to me, or at least a little goofy.

KAREN: I don't see why. Think of how painful it is to see a friend in a hospital bed even if you know he'll recover. And then remember that Lazarus wasn't just sick, he was dead. Jesus was surrounded by grieving friends while another friend lay dead in a tomb. I think he would have been cold-hearted not to get emotional.

PAUL: Then what about losing his temper? He got angry more than once. He even destroyed private property in the temple. I would expect God to be more of a model citizen.

KAREN: You should read Thoreau's essay on civil disobedience. There are times when righteous indignation is appropriate.

PAUL: Thoreau spent some time in jail, as I recall, because he wouldn't pay his taxes. Is that a piece of God-like behavior?

KAREN: Thoreau was protesting the use of his tax money for what he thought was an unjust war. I won't try to defend his position on policy, but I think it shows that defying authority is sometimes understandable. That was certainly true when Jesus overturned the tables in the temple.

PAUL: But tearing up the temple led to his death. He knew that would happen, and he did it anyway. That is suicidal. I think suicide is a symptom of crazy, don't you?

KAREN: There is a difference between suicide and sacrifice. The men who stormed the beaches on D-day sacrificed their lives to stop Hitler's Nazis. Were they crazy?

PAUL: I think I need to change tactics. You can't deny Jesus got angry more than once. Isn't anger a sin? I thought Jesus was sinless.

KAREN: Anger itself is not a sin. The Bible says not to let the sun go down on your anger. In other words, you will get angry sometimes—sometimes it is justified—just don't let it take over your life. Get angry if you must, but get over it. That is just what Jesus did. He got angry sometimes, but didn't stay that way for long.

PAUL: Bad temper or not, you have to admit Jesus sounded a little paranoid. He had delusions of his own greatness, and thought people were out to get him. That is classic paranoia.

KAREN: He wasn't delusional about his greatness if he was God. How do you get any greater than that?

PAUL: But he ran around saying people wanted to kill him. They kept saying "What are you talking about? Who wants to kill you?" Jesus saw things that weren't there.

KAREN: He saw things that weren't there *yet*. But they were coming. Being aware of real dangers around you is not paranoia, it is perception. Jesus was very perceptive. As you might expect from an all-knowing God.

PAUL: You had to work in that last part, didn't you?

KAREN: I just state the facts. I can't help it if they support my position.

PAUL: You state the facts as you see them. But the fact is that some people of his time thought Jesus was a lunatic, or possessed by demons. Those were the opinions of people who saw him every day. They would have a better grasp of his situation than we can, two thousand years later.

KAREN: Some people in George Washington's time thought he was a traitor to his country when he fought against England. Does that mean we should view him now as a traitor?

PAUL: We wouldn't now, of course, because he won. Winners get to write history the way they see it. But from the perspective of many people at the time, he was a traitor. How do you know the folks who thought Jesus was crazy didn't have a more accurate perspective than those who thought he was sane?

KAREN: I will admit that some people thought Jesus was crazy. They were mostly the phony religious leaders like you mentioned earlier. They thought he was crazy because they didn't want to believe he was who he said he was. They had the most to lose, so they were the hardest to convince. Trying to get through to them would be like me trying to teach a pig to sing. It would waste my time, and irritate the pig.

PAUL: You just can't help being colorful, can you?

KAREN: It's a gift.

102

PAUL: I'll withhold judgment on that. What do you think of the idea that Jesus had a sound mind, but false motives? He may have simply deceived everyone around him.

KAREN: If he did, then he was the greatest deceiver of all time. What possible motive would he have for claiming to be God? He knew he would be persecuted and killed for making a statement like that.

PAUL: I don't know what his motives were, but if he wasn't crazy, then he must have been a liar. There is no other explanation for what he said.

KAREN: There is one other explanation.

PAUL: I could see that one coming. Your explanation is that if he wasn't crazy, and wasn't a liar, then he must have been who he said he was.

KAREN: Excellent deductive reasoning.

PAUL: Thanks, but I have another objection.

KAREN: Let's have it.

PAUL: If Jesus was God, why was he such a bore?

KAREN: A bore? Jesus? You must be joking. I think he would have been a blast to spend time with.

PAUL: A blast? Come on. Watch the old movies about him. He never cracks a smile. Neither do any of the people around him. Every conversation is a God-like pronouncement. I can just see people slowly moving away from him, rolling their eyes as they sneak away. Jesus must have been the most boring person in the Roman Empire.

KAREN: Movies are probably not the best way to investigate the life of Jesus. The written accounts clearly show that people wanted to be around him. He was invited to the wedding in Cana, remember?

PAUL: How is that significant?

KAREN: He probably wouldn't have been invited if he was a bore. He was invited because people enjoyed his company. He must have had a tremendous amount of charisma. Men and women left their homes and families just to be near him. They wouldn't do that for a bore. I think he loved to laugh, tell stories, and share a good meal with friends. He probably even danced at the wedding. Jesus was a lot of things, but boring wasn't on the list.

PAUL: I never thought of it that way. But even if everything you say is true, it doesn't really prove Jesus was God in human form. It is all circumstantial evidence. It all requires reasoning, deduction, an almost intuitive sorting of the facts. If Jesus wanted to show us he was

God, why didn't he give us conclusive proof? Why did he leave it open to question?

KAREN: I suppose because he has so much respect for our freedom. He gives us enough information to make a decision, and then lets us make it. Besides, he did give us one piece of solid evidence.

PAUL: Your definition of solid may be different from mine. What do you have?

KAREN: The one incident that proves Jesus was telling the truth. The resurrection.

PAUL: I was afraid you would come to that.

***

Gone and Back Again

KAREN: Do I detect skepticism on your part toward the resurrection?

PAUL: I'm skeptical about the Easter Bunny too. You don't really believe that Jesus died and came back to life three days later? How hokey is that?

KAREN: I've never heard the word hokey applied to the resurrection. But I believe it happened.

PAUL: I guess you can believe whatever you want. It doesn't really matter if it happened or not.

KAREN: It doesn't matter? Why not?

PAUL: Because it's the big picture that counts, not whether the resurrection actually happened. It's a great story either way. Overcoming difficulties, rising from the ashes, so to speak. The message of hope is there whether Jesus actually rose from the dead or not.

KAREN: So the resurrection means no more to you than the mythical story of the Phoenix.

PAUL: I like the story of the Phoenix. A bird with a beautiful voice dies and burns; then rises up singing again from its own ashes. The Phoenix rising tells the same story as the resurrection. Both messages give us hope.

KAREN: Hope in what? If Jesus didn't rise from the dead, what hope do you have? If Jesus didn't conquer death, as he said he would, then his message was a lie.

PAUL: You are missing the symbolism in the resurrection story. The story's message was of hope for the future. Rising above adversity. The story inspires hope whether Jesus actually rose or not.

KAREN: It doesn't inspire if it is a lie. I have no time for a symbolic resurrection story. The resurrection either happened or it didn't. If it did, then there is no more important event in human history.

PAUL: More important than the invention of frozen pizza? I guess I don't see it as that critical. As long as you get a positive message from the story, why does it matter if it really happened?

KAREN: It matters because Jesus did not suffer torture and humiliation on the cross so you would think positive thoughts. The resurrection was not that trivial. It was proof of Jesus' claim to be God. It elevates his words above all other philosophers and religious leaders. It changed the way we relate to God.

PAUL: How did it do that?

KAREN: We don't sacrifice doves and goats as atonement for our sins anymore, because Jesus sacrificed himself for us. That is why we call him the Lamb of God. He was the sacrificial lamb for the whole world.

PAUL: No kidding. I always thought you called him the Lamb of God because he was so meek and mild.

KAREN: Frankly, I don't see much in Jesus that is meek in the way you mean it. He was unpretentious, I suppose, but not timid. A timid man could not have faced crucifixion the way Jesus did.

PAUL: OK. Maybe he was a tough guy. Or maybe he was delusional. The jury is still out on that. But I don't see why it is so important to you that his resurrection was real. It's a great story, either way.

KAREN: The resurrection was a physical point of connection between God and man. It was a breathtaking example of how much God loves us. It is the center of all Christian thought. It can be none of those things unless it is an actual historical event.

PAUL: I hate to be the one to tell you, but it cannot be an actual historic event. Men don't stay dead for three days and then get up like they took an afternoon nap.

KAREN: I can't argue with you there. Men can't do that. But God can. And did.

PAUL: You may have become unhinged. This is the most unbelievable part of the whole Jesus story, and you are trying to defend it. It's a shame to see such a great mind wasted.

KAREN: Don't jump to any conclusions about my sanity. If you give me a minute, I may surprise you with a fact or two. You may even come around to my way of thinking.

PAUL: I doubt it, but I accept the challenge. Proceed as best you can.

KAREN: Let's start with what I think is the most important point. When the Romans crucified Jesus, his disciples abandoned him. They were afraid to admit they even knew him. Three days later they were ready to die to say he was God. They spent the rest of their lives being persecuted, tortured, and killed for telling that story, and not one of them ever denied it was true. Something happened to those people. Something so dramatic their lives were never the same. I believe it was the resurrection. What do you think it was?

PAUL: Maybe they had a mass hallucination or something. I don't know. Just because they all told this story doesn't mean it's true. People tell stories all the time. My Grandpa used to tell me how he saved his neighbor's life by pulling him out of a burning house.

KAREN: I remember your Grandpa. That seems a little out of character for him.

PAUL: You're right. It turns out that Grandpa set the fire. I never did find out for sure why. Something to do with insurance, I imagine.

KAREN: Delightful man, your Grandpa.

PAUL: Grandpa had his faults, but he could get your attention when he started to spin a tale. Maybe Jesus' followers were just good storytellers, like Grandpa.

KAREN: Your Grandpa never let the truth get in the way of a good story. Jesus' followers didn't have that luxury. They were compelled to tell the truth, and spent years and years telling it, even though they were stoned and tortured for it. They wouldn't have done that for a lie. Jesus' disciples were telling the truth.

PAUL: They may have very well believed the story was true. That goes back to the hallucination theory. If they wanted to see a risen Jesus so badly, they might have seen him as an illusion brought on by their despair.

KAREN: Illusions don't eat breakfast. Hallucinations don't tell people to touch the holes in their hands, or hold lengthy conversations with different people at different times. Jesus did all three.

PAUL: Then maybe he didn't die on the cross. Maybe he just passed out from the heat and thirst. He could have relaxed in that cool dark cave for a couple of days and then walked out.

KAREN: I have heard that theory. In order to believe it, you have to ignore details of the eyewitness accounts.

PAUL: How do you mean?

KAREN: Remember that crucifixion was the most painful way imaginable to die. The Romans drove spikes through wrists and feet and then lifted the body in the air, nailed to the cross. The victim would hang in the sun for hours. They lost so much fluid from sweat and blood that thirst was overwhelming. The experience was so painful they had to make up a new word to describe it. The pain of crucifixion is what led to the word "excruciating".

PAUL: So it was painful. Extremely painful. That doesn't mean Jesus died from it.

KAREN: Romans weren't in the habit of letting people live through a crucifixion. A soldier who let a sentenced man survive was punished with death himself.

PAUL: Are you telling me no one ever survived crucifixion? No one?

KAREN: I can't say for certain that no one ever survived a crucifixion, but I know Jesus didn't.

PAUL: How can you be so sure?

KAREN: For one thing, because they didn't break his legs.

PAUL: You seem to be talking in riddles.

KAREN: Pardon me. Sometimes I get in a hurry to get to the point and I skip the important parts. Think about what caused death on the cross. A man's wrists were nailed to a beam above his head, so his entire body weight hung from his arms. As his upper torso stretched and tightened from the weight, it was nearly impossible to expand his chest. In other words, he couldn't breathe. The victim would lift himself up with his legs, painful as that was, to take the pressure off his chest, so he could take in air. As he grew too weak to lift himself, he slowly suffocated.

PAUL: And they broke his legs so he couldn't lift himself?

KAREN: Exactly. The Romans only had so much patience. If a man didn't die quickly enough to suit them, they would break his legs so he couldn't lift himself to breathe. You don't live long if you can't breathe. You may remember from the gospel accounts that they didn't break Jesus' legs. Do you know why?

PAUL: I'll bet you do.

KAREN: Because he was already dead. They didn't have to bother.

PAUL: Wait a minute. Let's assume for the sake of argument that he didn't die. He just passed out from the pain, and they thought he was dead. If the Romans didn't break his legs, then it would have been easier for him to get out of the tomb when he woke up. I remember reading that he didn't hang on the cross very long. Maybe he didn't suffer as much as you think. Maybe he didn't really die. Maybe it was a hoax.

KAREN: It is hard to believe that when you consider everything that happened that day. Remember that Jesus was beaten nearly to death by the Roman soldiers before he ever reached the cross. You should remember too that when the guards pierced Jesus' side with a spear, blood and water ran out. That is exactly what it would have looked like if the heart had failed, because fluid would have filled the membrane around the heart, and around the lungs.

PAUL: I was just getting ready to order a sandwich. You're not helping my appetite.

KAREN: Sorry. You asked for the facts.

PAUL: The fact is that if he survived the crucifixion, he could have walked out of the tomb. The disciples would have been amazed to see him. They probably would have thought he was God.

KAREN: I doubt if they would have been too inspired by a bloody, half-dead invalid. Besides, how could he have moved the stone that blocked the entrance to the tomb? You have to give up these crazy theories. Jesus died on the cross.

PAUL: Maybe. But your witnesses were fisherman and farmers two thousand years ago. They would be a lot easier to fool than we are.

KAREN: Could be, but dead is dead, whether it's now or the first century. I suspect farmers and fishermen could recognize a corpse as easily as we can. And I don't think it was any more common in Jesus' time to come back to life after three days in the tomb.

PAUL: That raises the second point. Even if Jesus died, how can you be so sure he came back?

KAREN: You are not trotting out the hallucination theory again are you?

PAUL: No, I'll concede that hallucinations don't eat breakfast. But I can't get past the possibility that the apostles just made the whole thing up.

KAREN: Why would they do that?

PAUL: Maybe they wanted to start a new religion, or maybe they wanted to travel the country living off the stories they could tell. It sounds like a pretty easy life to me.

KAREN: It takes a devious mind to come up with a theory like that.

PAUL: Yeah, I should have been a spy.

KAREN: Or a fiction writer. The easy life you imagine for the apostles is the opposite of what they lived. They were devout Jews who were no longer welcomed by most of their fellow Jews. They were persecuted by the Romans. They were stoned to death, jailed, tortured, and crucified. It would have been the easiest thing in the world to stop telling the story, but none of them did. None of them ever stopped telling the story of Jesus' resurrection.

PAUL: It is still possible that the whole thing was a conspiracy among the apostles.

KAREN: The conspiracy theory goes against everything we know about human nature. Look at the scandal that brought down President Nixon. He and about ten close advisors conspired to cover up the Watergate break-in during Nixon's reelection campaign. They were the most powerful people in the world. If any group of men in the world should have been able to pull off a conspiracy, it was them. Yet they couldn't hold a lie together for more that a few months when their self-interest was threatened. Their conspiracy collapsed at the first hint of danger. That is human nature, and the nature of conspiracies.

PAUL: Maybe the twelve disciples were the exception. They may have worked out the most successful conspiracy in history.

KAREN: Why would they conspire to lie? They had nothing to gain, and everything to lose, by telling that lie. These farmers and fisherman that you have so little respect for never recanted, through torture and persecution. They had no power or influence, yet they changed the world. Pretty impressive, don't you think?

PAUL: Impressive, yes. But just because they convinced a lot of people to believe the resurrection story doesn't mean it's true.

KAREN: There are only two possibilities. Either the resurrection is an actual historical fact or it is not. The witnesses said Jesus died on the cross and rose from the dead three days later, just as he predicted he would.

If there was no conspiracy, no lies, and no hallucination, what other explanation do you have?

PAUL: It just seems to me that God would find a method to show his power that wasn't so gross. A bloody corpse and all, you know? Why wouldn't he use something more spiritual or supernatural to show he's boss? Or a huge fireworks display or something?

KAREN: The Old Testament is full of signs and wonders that most of the world ignored. Maybe God thought it was time to communicate on a more personal level. Maybe he wanted to give us an illustration of what a righteous man should be. Maybe the death and resurrection of a man is the most intimate example of his power. Whatever his reasons for causing it to happen, I believe the story of the resurrection is true.

PAUL: I'm afraid you are like most people. You believe it because you were taught it as a child. Your preconceived notions lead you to believe what you want to believe. Your opinion is tainted.

KAREN: If that is true, then I suppose no one has a valid opinion about anything, because everybody has preconceived notions. That would include you. Maybe your preconceived notions lead you to believe what you want to believe.

PAUL: You love to use my own words against me, don't you?

KAREN: Not especially. I just want to make sure our opinions are judged with the same criteria. By the way, I was not taught to believe in the resurrection. I considered it a myth for most of my life.

PAUL: You surprise me. It's rare to find an intelligent person who became a Christian as an adult.

KAREN: A while ago, you told me I was insulting. I think you just turned the tables.

PAUL: It is not meant to be an insult, just an observation.

KAREN: I will try to take it that way, but I think your observation is incorrect. You might be surprised how many Christians came to faith the same way I did.

PAUL: How is that?

KAREN: I became an atheist in college, more out of a sense of superiority than any real strength of belief. I used to quote Mark Twain, who said, "Faith is believing what you know ain't so." I thought that's what faith was. I dabbled in philosophy, eastern religions, New Age mysticism. None of it seemed real to me. None of it sounded really true. I even read the New Testament looking for information I could use to argue with Christians. That's a dangerous thing to do if you want to stay an atheist.

PAUL: Don't tell me those sneaky Christians got the best of you in an argument. You must be slipping.

KAREN: An argument is only as good as the information behind it. Christians had better information than I did. I had opinions, relativism, and the kind of tolerance that would allow no other view. Christians had truth, love, and acceptance of me with all my faults. I was shocked.

PAUL: I'm shocked that your opinions could be so easily changed.

KAREN: I never said it was easy. I doubt if there was ever a more unwilling convert than me. I didn't want to submit to the authority of God. I liked being the ultimate authority myself, but I have always tried to be intellectually honest. I tend to accept the truth, whether or not it matches my personal preferences. I could no longer reject the Christian story once I became convinced it was true.

PAUL: Part of the truth you accepted was the literal resurrection of Jesus?

KAREN: It was the most important point. Once I realized Jesus' resurrection was a real historical fact, I became fascinated with the whole Christian story. That is when the hard part started.

PAUL: What was so hard?

KAREN: I began to realize I was not the center of the universe. That was hard. I liked being the center of the universe.

PAUL: I'm almost afraid to continue this conversation.

KAREN: Why?

PAUL: I like being the center of the universe too. The more we talk, the more I wonder if I am.

KAREN: You can't fight progress.

***

The First Four

PAUL: If uncertainty is progress, then we have come a long way. But there is something I think you're confused about too, whether you realize it or not.

KAREN: The world is full of things that confuse me. Which one do you have in mind?

PAUL: The eyewitness accounts of Jesus' life you keep referring to. I presume you mean the four gospels?

KAREN: Matthew, Mark, Luke, and John.

PAUL: You realize, of course, those gospels have been pretty much discredited as historical sources.

KAREN: You interest me, young man. How have they been discredited?

PAUL: Lots of ways. First of all, they probably weren't even written by Matthew, Mark, Luke and John. They are full of inconsistencies and errors. And no other writers of the time claimed Jesus was the messiah. You would think the Son of God would have gotten some press—if the story really happened.

KAREN: Wow. I don't mean to sound too abrupt, my friend, but you are stunningly misinformed.

PAUL: I don't think so. Everything I said is pretty much common knowledge.

KAREN: It used to be common knowledge that the world was flat, but I haven't heard of anybody falling off the edge lately.

PAUL: You chose a poor analogy there. Books about a carpenter rising from the dead fall in the same category as the flat-earth theory.

KAREN: Not really. I think there is a stronger case for the gospels than against them.

PAUL: You can't deny the gospels look suspicious. Sections of Matthew and Luke were obviously copied from Mark. These guys couldn't even make up their own stories.

KAREN: Sections of the first three gospels appear to come from a common source. I don't see how that proves they aren't true.

PAUL: It shows they were just repeating whatever stories they were told. Eyewitnesses don't have to do that. Counterfeiters do.

KAREN: Strong words. But not appropriate, in my view. The fact that you study from a classmate's notes doesn't prove you were absent from class. The gospels don't seem phony to me just because parts of them are very similar.

PAUL: Then what about all the inconsistencies? Why do some of the gospels go on at length about Jesus' birth, and some don't even bring it up? Three of the gospels don't even mention turning water into wine. How could they miss that? How can you trust an eyewitness who ignores the very first miracle?

KAREN: You can't seem to make up your mind what to complain about. First it's the gospels' similarities, and now it's their differences. You are like Goldilocks, only nothing is ever just right. The bed is always too hard or too soft. What would it take to please you?

PAUL: A reasonable amount of similarity. Agreement on the main points, and enough details to show the authors saw the same things. For instance, Jesus had to be born in Bethlehem to fulfill Biblical prophecy, so that is stuck in Matthew. His birth isn't even mentioned in some of the gospels. Why would they leave out such an important point if they were valid histories?

KAREN: I'm not sure the gospel writers set out to write complete histories of Jesus' life. I think they wrote what they felt strongly about, or to the audience they wanted to reach. Matthew wrote to the Jews, Luke to the Gentiles. Mark was technical, John was theological. They wrote from their own perspective. It is not surprising they stressed different points. It's like the summer my brother and I stayed with my grandparents when we were teenagers. We both wrote letters home, about the same summer, and the same grandparents, but we talked about completely different things. That is human nature. It didn't mean our parents couldn't trust our letters to be true and accurate.

PAUL: I doubt if there was any question that you and your brother were really at your grandparents' house. And they knew you wrote the letters. But there is no way to know who wrote the gospels after all this time. Just look at the controversy about who wrote Shakespeare's plays. I read the other day that some scholars think Shakespeare didn't write them at all. They think Christopher Marlowe wrote them, or the Earl of Oxford. Mark Twain thought Francis Bacon wrote them. Shakespeare lived just a few hundred years ago, and we can't agree who wrote his plays. How can you be sure who wrote the gospels when they were written two thousand years ago?

KAREN: I can't claim to know who wrote the Shakespeare plays, although I suspect Shakespeare didn't. For the same reasons I believe the gospels were probably written by the men they were named for.

PAUL: I'm always a little nervous about asking for your reasons.

KAREN: Why is that?

PAUL: Because you always give them to me.

KAREN: Aren't you lucky to have a friend so willing to share?

PAUL: It's a mixed blessing. So now you're an expert on Shakespeare too?

KAREN: I don't know that I'm an expert on anything. I just like to get my facts straight, and then make a judgment without getting too emotional about it.

PAUL: Then give me your cold-blooded judgment. Who wrote what?

KAREN: You have to apply the same logic to both questions. Whoever wrote the Shakespeare plays had extensive knowledge of the military, the sea, the king's court, and most of all, the law. There is no evidence that William Shakespeare spent time in any of those areas. If you look at the verifiable facts of his life, it is hard to see how he could have known enough about those subjects to write convincingly. The Gospel writers, on the other hand, were in the best possible position to know Jesus' story. They were either eyewitnesses or close associates of men who were.

PAUL: That's interesting, but a bit flimsy. What else do you have against old Will?

KAREN: Look at the people who knew him. The good folks in Stratford took no notice of William Shakespeare. There were no diary entries about how they bumped into the great man at the butcher shop. There were no eulogies about how a brilliant playwright was gone when he died. That's hard to understand if he was really the most famous author of his time. They knew him, but he was no more important to them than the local blacksmith.

PAUL: I see the connection you're trying to make. The people of Shakespeare's time had the best chance to know if he really wrote the plays. The early Christians had the best chance to know who wrote the gospels.

KAREN: Your line of reasoning is sound. What conclusion does it lead you to?

PAUL: I think it is your line of reasoning leading me to a conclusion, but here it is. Since the early Christians thought the gospels were named for their real authors, it is probably true.

KAREN: Good call.

PAUL: Let's assume they were right, and that Mark and Luke really wrote their gospels. Mark and Luke spent no time with Jesus. How do you count them as eyewitnesses?

KAREN: The early church was clear that John Mark was a close companion of Peter the apostle. Peter was certainly part of Jesus' inner circle. John Mark recorded Peter's accounts in the Gospel of Mark. Luke was Paul's companion and "beloved physician." He was also an historian. He wrote the Gospel of Luke, and the book of Acts.

PAUL: Paul was the Jew who Jesus struck blind for three days on the road to Damascus, right?

KAREN: He was more than that. He was one of the Jews who persecuted and killed Christians. Until he met Jesus. Then his life changed.

PAUL: But Paul didn't witness Jesus' life. Jesus was dead in the ground before Paul was ever converted.

KAREN: In the ground for three days, anyway. But Paul saw the risen Jesus, and met with the apostles in Jerusalem shortly after his conversion. Luke would have had the perfect opportunity to research the story and write it down.

PAUL: So Luke got his information second hand. That doesn't sound all that reliable to me. Even eyewitnesses don't always agree. If ten people see a car crash, they will tell ten different stories about what they saw.

KAREN: I suppose the details would be a little different, but they would all report they saw a wreck. It's like that fight we saw in Mr. Elmore's English class. Remember?

PAUL: Sure. Mr. Elmore staged a fight between two seniors, right in the middle of a discussion on the shortcomings of Ernest Hemingway. Everybody in class thought it was a real fight. Including you.

KAREN: It was the most excited I ever got in an English class.

PAUL: Me too. I was hoping to see a little blood, but it was over too soon. Then Mr. Elmore ran into the room and told us to write down what we had seen.

KAREN: And everybody wrote something a little different.

PAUL: That was the point of the exercise, as I recall. To show that eyewitnesses are not reliable. Haven't you just proved my point for me?

KAREN: Not exactly. Didn't everybody write that the seniors got in a fight? Did anybody miss the main point of the event? Of course not. We may have missed a few of the minor details, but everybody knew two guys were rolling around on the floor trying to bludgeon each other. It's the same with the gospel witnesses. They didn't include every single detail of Jesus' story. They didn't need or want to. But they didn't miss the main event. Neither did Luke.

PAUL: You are wearing me down. I suppose you can defend Matthew as an eyewitness author as well.

KAREN: All I can tell you is that Matthew was a tax collector. They were pretty much hated in those days, so it wouldn't have made much sense to use his name unless he really was the author of the gospel.

PAUL: How come?

KAREN: If you were going to name a false author, you would choose someone the readers admired or trusted. Being a tax collector, Matthew was neither. So they wouldn't have named him as an author unless he really was.

PAUL: What about the Gospel of John? You will surely admit there is some question about who wrote it.

KAREN: There is some question about which John actually wrote it. An early Christian historian mentioned a "John the Elder" in association with the book. Whether he meant the apostle John or a different John is not completely clear. My personal opinion is that the Gospel of John is eyewitness testimony.

PAUL: Personal opinion? I thought you dealt only in absolute truth. Don't tell me you base your faith on opinion. I'm disappointed.

KAREN: Cheer up. It's not as bad as it sounds. The Gospel of John agrees on nearly all points with the other three Gospels. If you read some of the books not accepted in the Bible, like the Gospel of Philip, or Mary, or James, they are filled with stories that were obviously invented and exaggerated. John isn't like that. It reads like an eyewitness account.

PAUL: But John presents a different picture of Jesus than the other Gospels. John spends a lot more time talking about Jesus as God.

KAREN: The view of Jesus as God is more clearly spelled out in John, but it is in all the Gospels.

PAUL: So all the gospel writers were trying to sell the idea of Jesus as God?

KAREN: I guess that is one way to put it.

PAUL: Then you can't trust any of them. If all the Gospel writers were trying to sell us on the idea that Jesus was God, then that opens them all up to suspicion. They wrote with a specific goal in mind, like a salesman writing a cigarette ad. How can you trust that?

KAREN: You are very cynical for one so young.

PAUL: I have reason to be. Listen, at one time, the Japanese wrote Pearl Harbor out of their history books. They were trying to sell the idea of their historical innocence. American history books used to do the same thing with the story of our treatment of the Native Americans. How do you know the gospel writers didn't distort the facts the same way to sell their idea of a messiah?

KAREN: I don't doubt they had a goal in mind. They wanted to spread the word about Jesus. But they had nothing to gain from making up stories about Him. Think of how radical their story was. How revolutionary their practices seemed at the time. They changed dietary laws that had been in effect for centuries. They changed rules of sacrifice and worship that their contemporaries thought would send them straight to Hell. They changed the Sabbath from Saturday to Sunday, because that is the day Jesus rose. Let me remind you what they got from all of this. They were tortured, persecuted, hounded and killed. But they never gave up. People will not behave this way for what they know is a lie, and the eyewitnesses had the best opportunity to know if the Jesus story was a lie. It was true, and they recorded it as the truth.

PAUL: Then why didn't anybody else talk about Jesus at the time? Why are the gospels the only record we have of Jesus?

KAREN: They aren't. The Roman historian Tacitus mentioned Jesus in his writings. So did Joesephus. Have you heard of him?

PAUL: I may not be as misinformed as you think. Joesephus was a Jewish historian who lived about the same time as Jesus. He wasn't too popular with the Jews, because he cozied up to the Romans.

KAREN: Cozied up to the Romans? You sound like a cheap detective novel.

PAUL: Sorry. Once in a while I get colorful. Joesephus was kind of a rat, but he wrote a pretty complete history of the Jews. Without saying Jesus was the Messiah, by the way.

KAREN: Let me be clear. I never claimed Joesephus thought Jesus was the Messiah. He probably didn't. But Joesephus did say that others thought Jesus was the Messiah. He did say Jesus was crucified and reportedly rose from the dead. The point to remember here is that there are references to Jesus outside the Gospels.

PAUL: I'll say this for you. You are consistent in your position. But you know what Emerson said, "Consistency is the hobgoblin of little minds."

KAREN: Actually, he said, "A foolish consistency is the hobgoblin of little minds." You wouldn't call me foolish, would you?

PAUL: How about stubborn?

KAREN: I can live with that.

***

Fact or Fiction?

PAUL: You sound like most Christians—far too rigid about the books you read. The first four gospels may be important books, but they are not the only books.

KAREN: You sound like you have a book or two in mind.

PAUL: Absolutely. And with your sense of curiosity on the subject, I'm surprised you haven't extended your reading list.

KAREN: You may be surprised at my reading list. What books are you referring to?

PAUL: To start with, the Gospel of Thomas. Or as it is affectionately known, The Fifth Gospel.

KAREN: Ah, yes. The Gospel of Thomas. The favorite of New Age mystics and liberal seekers of truth.

PAUL: And rejected by small-minded fundamentalists. Thomas doesn't reflect your rigid view of Jesus, so you don't believe it. You fall prey once again to your preconceived notions. You believe what you want to believe.

KAREN: I guess that charge could be tossed your direction as well. As I recall, The Gospel of Thomas makes Jesus look more like a guru than a savior. It seems to me it would be just what a lot of people would want to hear. Wisdom without redemption, spirituality without sacrifice, self-reliance without God.

PAUL: You make that sound like it's a bad thing. You're just like the mainstream church. It doesn't like the idea of a user-friendly Jesus. That's why religious scholars were afraid to investigate Jesus until the last fifty years or so. They didn't want to end up like Galileo.

KAREN: You mean dying peacefully in bed at a ripe, old age?

PAUL: I mean persecuted by the church for heresy.

KAREN: That is a bit overblown, I think. Galileo probably wasn't too happy with his treatment at the hands of the church, but he wasn't tortured or killed. Neither were any religious scholars for the last century or so. The search for a less demanding Jesus has been around for a long time, not just the last fifty years.

PAUL: But modern scholarship started around 1950. That's when they found ancient scrolls in Egypt and Palestine.

KAREN: You are talking about the Dead Sea Scrolls and the texts at Nag Hammadi?

PAUL: Right. They contained the Gospel of Thomas and boatloads of other texts. Did you ever wonder why they were buried in the desert?

KAREN: I can't understand why I do the things I do, let alone somebody stuffing scrolls in a cave fifteen hundred years ago.

PAUL: Don't try to get clever with me. You're always the one to reason everything out. You know very well they buried those texts because they were afraid the church would destroy them.

KAREN: Why would the church do that?

PAUL: Because it had a vested interest in keeping the first four gospels as the only truth. It kept everyone under the thumb of the church hierarchy. They didn't want a new gospel out there that let people think for themselves.

KAREN: Is it possible they wanted to maintain the first four gospels as the true story of Jesus simply because those books told the truth?

PAUL: I think their motives were a little less pure than that.

KAREN: I know your opinion of their motives. The question was: Is it possible they believed the first four gospels were closer to the truth than the rest of the texts?

PAUL: Of course it is possible. It is just highly un-likely. The church has too long a history of persecution to believe otherwise.

KAREN: Are you saying persecution by the church proves the first four gospels were not true? I don't see the connection.

PAUL: If the church persecuted anybody who dis-agreed with them, they must not have paid much at-tention to the gospels. They didn't love their neighbors a whole lot.

KAREN: Are you saying their disregard of the mes-sage proves the gospels are not true?

PAUL: You clamp down on a question like a pit bull. You just can't let something go.

KAREN: I find that I understand things a lot better if I settle one question before I fog up my mind with another.

PAUL: Then let's clear the fog on this one. If the early church used torture and intimidation to enforce their views on the truth, which they did, then their mo-tives are suspect, as is their judgment. If these are the best guys you can find to decide which gospel is true, you are in sad shape indeed.

KAREN: Their methods were suspect, certainly. Their motives are harder to criticize. They were trying to bring the message of Christ to the masses.

PAUL: So the early priests would either save you or send you to Hell?

KAREN: You are being too simplistic.

PAUL: And you are being too sensitive. You get that way when you can't defend your position.

KAREN: It is hard to defend torture, and there is no doubt some of that occurred in the church's past, but I can't leap to your conclusion that it proves the gospels false, or Thomas true.

PAUL: Scholars have recognized Thomas as a legitimate gospel for years. One of the reasons is because it was written so soon after Jesus died. The first four gospels were written years after Jesus lived, so they may not reflect what the early Christians believed. All of Christianity may be a colossal mistake.

KAREN: That is a colossal conclusion to draw from one little book. And you should be aware that only a very small group of biblical scholars take that position on Thomas. Small, but vocal.

PAUL: I will draw my own conclusions, thank you. The first four gospels were written centuries after Jesus lived. Who knows what kind of myths developed in that length of time? Myths like Jesus claiming to be God, or rising from the dead. How do you know those weren't just stories developed over time, like Benjamin Franklin flying a kite in a thunderstorm?

KAREN: Benjamin Franklin did fly a kite in a thunderstorm.

PAUL: All right, but you get my point. Exaggerations grow over time. Myths develop. How do you know that didn't happen with Jesus?

KAREN: I'm glad you asked that, because that accusation has always bothered me. There is a lot of controversy about when the gospels were written. Obviously, the closer to Jesus' time, the more accurate they can be assumed to be.

PAUL: Sure. And the Gospel of Thomas was written before the first four gospels.

KAREN: There lies the controversy. Very few experts place the date of Thomas ahead of the four gospels. Most scholars would tell you the gospels were written within the lifetime of eyewitnesses who could have completely discounted the stories, and they weren't discounted. As for the myths developing over time, that is easy to disprove. Some of Paul's letters were written within a few years of Jesus' crucifixion, and he said Jesus was God, He died for our sins, and rose from the grave. These were not myths that developed over time. They were the basic beliefs of Christians right after Jesus' death.

PAUL: We are back to Paul again. Paul the persecutor who turned preacher. Didn't he write about a third of the Christian Bible?

KAREN: Paul's letters make up about a third of the New Testament, if that's what you mean.

PAUL: That's what I mean. The New Testament is basically the story of Jesus and the early Christian church, most of it from Paul's perspective. How do you know Paul didn't make up the story of the risen Jesus? Maybe the gospel writers just repeated what Paul said, whether it was true or not.

KAREN: That sounds like another conspiracy theory. What possible motivation did Paul have to do that? Have you read his letters?

PAUL: Sure, I read them. I don't deny they are well written. A bit close-minded, but generally a positive message. But that doesn't mean he didn't make it all up.

KAREN: I am glad you got something positive out of it. But you must have ignored the part about how Paul went to prison and got chained to the wall of a cell. He escaped murder in the middle of the night for preaching the gospel story. It's hard to imagine he went through all that just to make up a fairy tale. The Brothers Grimm wrote fairy tales. Do you think they would have put up with time in jail to tell their stories?

PAUL: Maybe for Hansel and Gretel. That's a good one.

KAREN: I especially like the part where the old witch gets cooked in her own oven.

PAUL: That's drama, all right. Sometimes it's good to relax with a little pure fiction.

KAREN: Like the Gospel of Thomas?

PAUL: You are too tough on Thomas. His gospel was written soon after Jesus' death, too.

KAREN: A great many people would disagree with you.

PAUL: Including you, I presume?

KAREN: Including me.

PAUL: So you listen to your experts, and I listen to mine. Who can say which group is right?

KAREN: Once again, you have to sift the facts from the hype. Look at the content of Thomas. It is just a collection of supposed Jesus sayings. No narrative. No story. What does that tell you?

PAUL: It tells me that Thomas was more of a journalist than a novelist. What does it tell you?

KAREN: A list of sayings would make no sense unless there was some context for it. That tells me that whoever wrote Thomas assumed the reader would already be clear on who Jesus was, and what happened to him.

PAUL: And how is that significant?

KAREN: If the reader already knew the Jesus story, then the gospels were already in existence. They must have been written before Thomas.

PAUL: That is clever. But even if they were written earlier, it doesn't prove they're more reliable.

KAREN: You already agreed the closer to Jesus' time they were written, the more accurate they probably were. You can't change the rules because your team is losing.

PAUL: But no matter when it was written, Thomas can still give us insights into Jesus' character.

KAREN: A gospel written years after Jesus died may tell us a lot about the beliefs of the time it was written, but I don't see how it can tell us much about Jesus. It's like the historical movies that come out occasionally. They give us insight into the director's opinion on history, but not a lot of historical fact.

PAUL: You know this fact, of course. The first four gospels were not legitimized until about the year 300. The Roman Emperor Constantine picked out the first four, and made the church go along with it. He could have just as easily picked out six or seven, and the whole idea of Christianity would have changed.

KAREN: I don't even like to call them the first four gospels. That makes it sound like there are other gospels that are just as valid. Not true.

PAUL: Call them what you like, if it weren't for Constantine, they wouldn't be so special.

KAREN: Your arguments are always well reasoned, well researched, and well spoken. But they have the distinct disadvantage of being wrong.

PAUL: Are you saying Constantine didn't gather a bunch of priests to validate his version of the New Testament?

KAREN: They didn't validate what was true as much as they rejected what was false. What was true was already pretty well known.

PAUL: It may have been pretty well known then, but the world has changed. Bookstores can't hold all the new gospels, and new views on the old ones. If there is no truth to the claims, why do they keep getting published?

KAREN: For the same reason cigarettes keep getting sold. Because somebody makes a profit from it. Biblical scholars are not immune to the pleasures of money and fame. And the more controversial the book, the more it sells. Books about codes hidden in scripture, revolutionary gospels suppressed by the church, murder, mayhem. Most of it is nonsense. But it sells.

PAUL: Maybe it sells because the new gospels are exciting. They are more inclusive of new ideas. They aren't as rigid and confining as the old-time religion. People don't want rules today. They want to feel good. They want to do their own thing. That is another reference to Emerson, by the way. "Do your own thing."

KAREN: I'm impressed. But I can't imagine anything more exciting than having a personal relationship with God. Doing your own thing seems pale by comparison.

PAUL: But doing your own thing is almost a religion itself these days. Like getting in touch with your inner spirit.

KAREN: Sad but true. Many people are looking for spirituality and inner peace. I guess they always have. It's just that there are more people selling phony versions of it these days. I think most seekers would be better off if they searched for truth, and questioned the motives of those who tell them what they want to hear.

PAUL: And you called me cynical. What about you?

KAREN: So far you have called me cynical, stubborn, consistent, and foolish. You are going to run out of adjectives soon.

PAUL: I have one more.

KAREN: I'm afraid to ask.

***

You're So Vain

PAUL: Stubborn, foolish, consistent, whatever you are, you can't deny a touch of arrogance.

KAREN: How is defending the Gospel story arrogant?

PAUL: Because it leads to the most outrageous claim that Christians make.

KAREN: Enlighten me on that, would you?

PAUL: Christians claim that Jesus is the only path to God. Jesus is the only way to eternal salvation, and everyone else is going straight to Hell.

KAREN: Have you ever heard a Christian actually say that?

PAUL: Let's say I gave you the condensed version.

KAREN: I guess you could condense Hamlet to "Something is rotten in Denmark," but I think you would miss some of the fine points of the story.

PAUL: Twist it around all you want, the facts remain. Christians claim they are right, and everybody else is wrong. Who are they to claim their faith is superior to every other one?

KAREN: I feel compelled to point out that Christians are not the only ones to make that claim.

PAUL: Who else claims exclusive truth the way Christians do?

KAREN: Hindus, for one.

PAUL: I have you there. Hindus are very tolerant. They easily accept Christian beliefs, or Islam, or just about anything else. They try to blend all beliefs together.

KAREN: Sure they do. As long as you accept their basic premises, which include the doctrines of karma and reincarnation. They won't bend on those. They claim those beliefs are true, and opposite beliefs are false. That sounds like exclusivity to me.

PAUL: You had better hope the law of karma isn't true. I know what you were like in high school. You have a lot to answer for.

KAREN: You were with me most of the time. I don't think the justice of karma is in your favor either.

PAUL: I guess we should both be looking over our shoulders if the Hindus are right, but I think you were a bad influence on me, rather than the other way around.

KAREN: There is no doubt I deserve a little moral retribution for my past acts. That's the great thing about Christianity. You don't get the punishment you deserve, and you get the mercy you don't.

PAUL: That's a seductive doctrine, I'll admit. But it doesn't eliminate the arrogance of your faith.

KAREN: Like the arrogance of a Muslim, who also claims to have exclusive truth? Or an atheist?

PAUL: An atheist? How is an atheist arrogant?

KAREN: They say every religion is wrong. All of them. One hundred per cent wrong. They claim they have a clearer insight into ultimate truth than the majority of people on earth. Only an atheist would have that kind of arrogance.

PAUL: At least they don't say you will go to eternal damnation if you don't believe them.

KAREN: That is only because they don't believe in eternal damnation. They usually have no problem saying a believer is naïve or childish. That was Freud's position.

148

PAUL: You don't intend to disagree with Sigmund Freud? Is nothing sacred to you?

KAREN: Many things are sacred to me. The opinions of Sigmund Freud are not on the list. He wasn't tolerant of Jews or Christians, or anybody else who believed in God. He thought they were delusional, and inferior to him. There is arrogance for you. I suspect a lot of atheists feel the same way. They just don't have the nerve to admit it.

PAUL: There is plenty of arrogance around, I suppose, but you have to admit you Christians are the worst.

KAREN: Is it more arrogant to believe you are a sinner in need of a savior, or that you are at the highest rung on the evolutionary ladder? Is it more arrogant to accept God, and bow down to a higher power, or to reject God and claim to be the ultimate being yourself?

PAUL: You are making atheists look pretty bad, but that is just a distraction from the issue. Christians say no one gets to the Father-God except through Jesus, right?

KAREN: That's pretty much the Christian belief. The question, though, was, "Is that arrogant?" Wasn't that the question?

PAUL: The answer is so self-evident, why even bother to respond? Of course it's arrogant. You say "Everybody who doesn't believe just the way I do is going to spend eternity in Hell." How could you be more arrogant than that?

KAREN: I don't doubt some Christians come off as arrogant. And that's a shame. They really don't mean for their message to sound that way.

PAUL: It sounds the way it is. Arrogant. Closed-minded. Superior.

KAREN: You can stop any time.

PAUL: You are not used to losing arguments, are you?

KAREN: I haven't lost the argument. I'm just taking a break to let you vent.

PAUL: Break time is over. Defend yourself.

KAREN: Here is a start. Christians are not arrogant because their message is available to everyone. You don't have to earn your way to salvation, or be at a particular economic level, or learn any secret gospel. Everybody is welcome. Christianity, it seems to me, is the least arrogant of all religions. It is completely open. Christians do believe, however, that where Christianity differs from other religions, the truth lies with them.

Christians simply believe what Jesus said, "I am the way and the truth and the life. No one comes to the father except through me."

PAUL: But that is open to interpretation. How do you know that Buddha wasn't another incarnation of Jesus, or that Hindus aren't going to Heaven? Jesus did say he had other flocks to attend to, didn't he? Didn't he say that?

KAREN: You've been peeking into a Bible again, haven't you? You'd better be careful. If you spend too much time in the word, you are liable to become a convert.

PAUL: Don't worry yourself too much about that. I just need enough information to straighten you out.

KAREN: Good luck.

PAUL: Thank you, but don't think you can duck the question. Didn't Jesus say he had other flocks to attend to?

KAREN: He did say that. Most people think what he meant by that was the Gentiles. He came first to the Jews, of course.

PAUL: Right. God's chosen people. That's the Jewish thing, isn't it?

KAREN: I don't think it's a Jewish thing. It's God's thing.

PAUL: Whatever. All I'm saying is that there are lots of methods to achieve spiritual enlightenment. There is meditation, philosophy, eastern religions. Christianity is not the only way.

KAREN: I won't argue with that, I guess. If all you are after is spiritual enlightenment, there are ways to find it. But maybe I should ask you what you mean by that.

PAUL: What? Spiritual enlightenment?

KAREN: Yes. I would like to know what you are trying to achieve. What do you mean by spiritual enlightenment?

PAUL: Getting in touch with the inner you. Finding inner peace. Lifting yourself above the mundane physical world.

KAREN: Those may be good starting points, but they're just the first step in a longer journey.

PAUL: The journey to God?

KAREN: Of course. Your spiritual journey is a walk in circles if it doesn't lead to the ultimate enlightenment. And that path is laid out by Jesus. Or rather through Jesus.

PAUL: Or maybe through Buddha, or Mohammed. Is your God so small that he can't show himself to other cultures without a Jewish carpenter? Maybe God reaches people however they need to be reached, whether it's through Islam, or Hinduism, or the Tao de Ching, or Confucius. Maybe those were the other flocks he was talking about. Maybe he uses whatever method is best for the individual he's trying to reach. Whatever fits their beliefs, their personality, their culture. That would allow them to find their own path to God. That makes much more sense to me.

KAREN: Because it makes more sense to you to reach people some other way, you choose to reject the message of Jesus. Is that right?

PAUL: I'm not sure I would phrase it that way. I'm not rejecting Jesus as much as I am accepting something else.

KAREN: That's a pretty fine distinction on which to risk eternity. Here is the problem with accepting those other beliefs, as I see it. The Bible says Jesus was God in human form. The other religions say he was not. Both statements cannot be true. All religions cannot be paths to the same god if they don't lead to the same place.

PAUL: Of course all religions have slightly different beliefs, but that doesn't mean they can't all lead to the same place. It is as if everyone in the country wanted to travel to Chicago. People in California would travel east. People in New York would travel west. They would be going in different directions, but arriving at the same destination. It is the same with different religions. They take different paths up the mountain, but they're all trying to reach the peak.

KAREN: I wish that were true, but it's not. Those folks trying to get to Chicago can only arrive in the same place if they know where that place is. If some of them think Chicago is in South Dakota, and some think it is Kansas, they may have a pleasant journey, but they will be surprised at the end. Since religions define their peak differently, they can't all get to the same one.

PAUL: But their peaks are not that different. The point of any religion you follow—if you get right down to the root of it—is to make you a better person, to make you relate to other people better, to make you kinder, gentler, all that stuff. Isn't that true? Won't any religion accomplish that? Won't any philosophy accomplish that? Because to have a better relationship with other people improves your life. It improves the world. How can you be against that? Look at Buddhism. Look at the Dali Lama. There isn't a kinder person in the world. He won't even kill a mosquito that bites him on the arm. How can you say that's wrong? Anybody who can get in touch with himself the way the Buddhists do will be better people. They will be more spiritually enlightened, more in touch with the universe. They are going to be better people. For culture, for society, how can that not be an improvement? How can you be opposed to that and not open yourself up to the charge of being arrogant?

KAREN: Calm down. You're about to break into song. My problem is with the way you frame the question. You presuppose that all beliefs are equal, and then ask me how I can say one is better than another. I say your premise is wrong. They are not all equal. They don't claim to be. Buddhism is not even a religion in the sense of worshipping God, because Buddhists don't believe in God. Buddhism is, at its core, an atheistic philosophy.

PAUL: Hold on. Even if they don't believe in God, don't they achieve some kind of spiritual enlightenment, and don't they treat people better than they would otherwise, and isn't that the main point of religion anyway?

KAREN: I don't know if your questions are getting more complicated or more confusing. Let me answer you with one word. No.

PAUL: No to what? No to which part of it?

KAREN: No to the question "Isn't the main point of religion to make people better to one another?" My answer is no. That is not the point of religion. The point of religion is to develop a relationship with God. To get back to the sacrifice on the cross for a moment, Jesus didn't come here to suffer humiliation and die nailed to a cross so people would be nice to each other. He came here to save people's souls. He came here to clear away our sins so we could have a personal relationship with a personal god. He didn't die so we would smile and say "Have a nice day."

PAUL: Wait a minute. Christians don't care if they are nice to one another? Being a good person isn't important to Christians?

KAREN: Sure it is. But being a nice person is not the main point of Christianity. Let me expand on that. The main point of Christianity is not social change, either. It's not to improve the plight of the poor. It's not to feed the hungry. It is not to save the environment. These are all side effects of Christianity, not its main point.

PAUL: I think a lot of Christians would disagree with you on that. What's the point of being a Christian if you don't care about doing good deeds?

KAREN: The point of Christianity is to love God, and to give your life to Christ. If you do that first, the good deeds will follow. My fear is that too many people use Christianity as a means to an end.

PAUL: I don't follow you.

KAREN: There are a lot of good people out there who get so wrapped up in their causes that they lose their perspective. Christianity becomes reduced to a method of justifying the cause, whether it is feeding children in Africa, or funding a political action committee.

PAUL: You seem to be saying that Christians don't need to get involved in social issues, or politics. You just accept Jesus, and then let somebody else solve the world's problems. I don't know if that's arrogant, or just dismissive.

KAREN: It's neither, because that's not what I said. Of course Christians should get involved. You can't just say a certain prayer or go to a particular church, and think your work is done. Christians are called to help others, and to be an example to others. I am just saying that having a relationship with God has to come first. Changing the world can be the result of—not the reason for—being a Christian.

PAUL: Don't tell me you think that calling yourself a Christian automatically makes you a good person.

KAREN: Calling yourself a Christian? No. But being a Christian certainly improves your odds. You don't have to tell a Christian not to murder or steal or gossip about their neighbors, because they don't want to anymore, or at least they know they shouldn't.

PAUL: Do you think the Dali Lama gossips about his neighbors?

KAREN: Having never been a neighbor of the Dali Lama, it's hard for me to say. Look, I don't doubt the Dali Lama is a wonderful human being. I'm sure most Buddhists are. So are most people who follow the teachings of Confucius or Mohammed. But I repeat that being a wonderful human being is not the point. The point of religious life, the point of life itself, is to have a relationship with God, and you do that through Jesus Christ.

PAUL: Are you saying Islamic people don't have a relationship with God? They pray, they read the Koran, they're devout. And what about Hindus? They don't have a relationship with God either?

KAREN: They are wading in the shallows of a very deep river.

PAUL: You have lapsed into metaphor. I hate metaphors.

KAREN: I felt a surge of inspiration.

PAUL: Try to restrain yourself. Your deep river is a connection with God?

KAREN: Right. I suggest that other religions contain some truth, but they're incomplete. Muslims like to be very structured in their worship, and feel they must earn their way to heaven. Hindus think they will be reincarnated and work their way to eventual oneness with the universe. Christianity is about salvation as a gift, paid for by another. Some people don't like that idea. It can be a difficult doctrine.

PAUL: How is salvation as a gift a difficult doctrine?

KAREN: We talked about the ugliness of the crucifixion. A lot of people don't like the idea of receiving salvation at the cost of murdering God. But the resurrection was the method God chose to prove Jesus' authority to speak the truth. Buddha didn't die and come back three days later. No Hindu ever did.

PAUL: Maybe no Hindu ever had to. Maybe Hindus can find the path to God without a bloody cross to show the way.

KAREN: We return to my earlier point. These religions cannot lead to the same God when they don't have the same concept of God. How can you defend such a position?

PAUL: It seemed pretty easy until I had a latte with you.

KAREN: I don't think the latte is your problem.

PAUL: My main problem is with your absolute conviction. Don't you ever have doubts? You are about as flexible as a granite statue.

KAREN: Am I not human? If you prick me, do I not bleed? Of course I have doubts. Who doesn't? Everyone questions their faith sometimes. And frankly, this is one of my least favorite topics related to my faith. I think we spend too much time worrying about the differences between religions instead of looking for what they have in common.

PAUL: At last. A reasonable statement. We should focus on what the different religions have in common. If everybody did that, there would be a lot less violence in the world.

KAREN: You are probably right. But I have to stand by my convictions. I've looked into the other religions, and the best evidence I can find leads to Christianity. I'm not going to fight anybody over it, or force anyone to agree with me, but I will remain a Christian.

PAUL: And you are convinced that this Christianity you're so proud of has had a positive impact on the world?

KAREN: Absolutely.

PAUL: I think it's time for a history lesson.

KAREN: Which one of us is the student?

PAUL: Get ready to take notes.

***

Holy Terror

PAUL: Somebody once said that there will always be good people doing good things, and bad people doing bad things, but for good people to do bad things, they need religion.

KAREN: That's a rather broad generalization.

PAUL: And like a lot of generalizations, it's based on the truth. Christianity has been used as an excuse for more bloodshed and slaughter than anything else you can imagine.

KAREN: I can name two worse things without even straining my imagination.

PAUL: Two things with a bloodier history than Christianity? I want to hear this.

KAREN: What about the Holocaust? That was about as bloody as you can get. The Nazis exterminated six million Jews.

PAUL: And your faithful Christians didn't do a thing about it. The church in Europe knew what was going on for years before the rest of the world did, and nobody heard a peep out of them. Do you know why? Because they made a pact with the devil. They knew Hitler would leave them alone if they kept quiet about his murdering the Jews, so they looked the other way. Is that part of your "love your neighbor" stuff?

KAREN: There is some evidence that the European church was silent about the Holocaust, just as you say. I believe the Pope publicly apologized for that.

PAUL: And that makes it OK? You let millions of people get killed, and then say "I'm sorry," and that makes you a good Christian? Face it. Your church history is riddled with hypocrisy. It has the blood of six million Jews on its hands.

KAREN: I don't think you can hold the Christian church responsible for the Holocaust. The Nazis perpetrated the atrocities, and they were not Christians.

PAUL: Germany was considered a Christian nation at the time. One of the best educated and enlightened countries in the world.

KAREN: Anybody can call themselves a Christian. It doesn't mean they really are.

PAUL: What are you saying? If the Germans had really been Christians, the Holocaust wouldn't have happened? Christians can do no wrong?

KAREN: Christians can certainly do wrong, and often do, but it is too easy to criticize the church, and not recognize the difference between the church and real Christians.

PAUL: Oh, that's interesting. If the church kills a few people here and there, it's not a real Christian's fault. It's just those darn phony Christians. How convenient for you.

KAREN: It is anything but convenient. Phony Christians make it easy for cynics to paint all Christians with the same brush, which seems unfair to me.

PAUL: So it's not fair to say the Germany that perpetrated the Holocaust was a Christian nation?

KAREN: What I am saying, I guess, is that the Nazi party was not a Christian organization. I recently read that they were more interested in occult practices. So although the church didn't do as much as it should have to stop it, the murder of those six million souls was done by non-Christians.

PAUL: With the complicity of Christians. Admit it. You are beaten.

KAREN: Bruised maybe, but not beaten.

PAUL: So your first example awards me a small victory. What is your second?

KAREN: Consider Joseph Stalin in Russia. He was worse than Hitler.

PAUL: I expected you to drag out old Joe. Stalin was one of the bad guys, that's for sure. But again, he did his evil deeds with no interference by the church.

KAREN: I don't know if that is true. I think the church did oppose Stalin, but he felt nothing but contempt. He said, "How many divisions has the Pope?"

PAUL: So he had no respect for the church. How do you figure he was worse than Hitler?

KAREN: It's not my figuring. It's common historical knowledge. Stalin wiped out intellectuals, professionals, transients, anybody he was suspicious of. He systematically eliminated all political opposition. He eventually became so paranoid that he killed his friends, just in case they might be plotting against him. I've heard estimates that he killed over 100 million people.

PAUL: That's a lot of dead Russians. But how does that let Christians off the hook for their own atrocities?

KAREN: You said Christianity was used as an excuse for the worst slaughters in history. I am just trying to show you that the worst atrocities in history were not committed by Christians.

PAUL: That's only because Christians didn't have gas chambers or gulags when they were in the mood to purge the populace. They did a pretty good job with the technology they had at hand. Besides, it's a flimsy argument to defend Christian cruelty by saying someone else did it too. That's like a fifth-grader who gets caught throwing rocks at the school window, and then points to her buddy hiding behind a bush, and saying, "He did it too."

KAREN: You have a long memory.

PAUL: You can't hide from the misdeeds of your past, and neither can your Christian heroes. They were a vicious bunch.

KAREN: So you keep saying. What is it about Christian history that you find so disturbing?

PAUL: I've already pointed out two cases where the church allowed murder and slaughter without raising a finger against it. That is enough to show the danger of religion, even if there was nothing else.

KAREN: But I'll bet there is something else.

PAUL: There is plenty, and you don't have to go across the Atlantic to find it. How do you feel about witch trials?

KAREN: Generally speaking, I'm opposed to them.

PAUL: I'm glad to hear it, but Christians in the eighteenth century weren't so kind. Apparently there wasn't enough excitement for them in Salem, Massachusetts back then, so they decided it would be amusing to torture and kill teenage girls. They called them witches and burned them alive.

KAREN: I don't think it was for their own amusement. They made the same mistake your doctors did when they bled people with leeches. They didn't really understand what they were doing.

PAUL: You are amazingly tolerant when it comes to Christian atrocities. Those people in Salem were pitiless tyrants. If a girl had a rash, or stuttered, or looked cross-eyed at a priest, they saw that as the work of the devil. Your Salem Christians weren't just evil, they were stupid, and those poor girls paid the price for that stupidity. Your religion smells of burning flesh. Your claims of piety are drowned out by the sound of screams.

KAREN: You are getting dramatic.

PAUL: You don't get much more dramatic than burning alive.

KAREN: The Salem witch trials were a black spot in Christian history, but they were sort of an isolated incident. They didn't last that long.

PAUL: Then let's consider something that did. How long did the Crusades last? Four hundred—five hundred years?

KAREN: Something like that.

PAUL: You don't seem that eager to talk about the Crusades. I can't say I'm surprised. Christians turned the Middle East into a slaughterhouse. They pulled women and children out of their homes, and murdered them in the streets. They cut the heads of anybody who they even suspected of not being Christian. They didn't just kill Muslims, they killed Jews too, and probably anyone else who didn't bow down to them. And what about the Inquisition? Killing people wasn't enough for Christians then. They tortured people to death. Put them on the rack. Slowly cut them in half. Drowned them. Or, if it was a slow day, they just beat them to death.

KAREN: Most of what you describe in the Inquisition was done by civil authorities, not the church.

PAUL: Don't give me that. The church was in charge, and you know it. How can you defend Christianity when it has a history like that?

KAREN: All I can say is that they thought they were doing the right thing. They thought they were saving souls.

PAUL: I am sure it was great comfort to the girls in Salem that the Christians who burned them alive were doing it out of love.

KAREN: Sarcasm is the lowest form of wit.

PAUL: It's hard to be witty about torturing children.

KAREN: Look, I can't defend the horrible acts you mentioned. Nobody can. But you have simply ignored the good works that Christians have done. Most hospitals in the United States are affiliated with a Christian denomination. The Salvation Army is a Christian group. Most of the Founding Fathers during the Revolution were Christians, and looked for divine guidance when they declared independence. Our country wouldn't even be here if it weren't for Christianity. Christians spearheaded the fight against slavery before the Civil War. Martin Luther King was a Christian pastor. We would have never had the Civil Rights movement without Christianity.

PAUL: Martin Luther King may have been a pastor, but I think it's a bit of a leap to say the Civil Rights movement would never have occurred without Christianity. You are straining logic to make a point.

KAREN: Here is the main point. You can come up with examples of terrible Christian history, and I can make the opposite argument. Whatever evidence you present, you can't conclude that Christianity is false because some Christians made some awful mistakes. Christianity did not fail. People failed.

PAUL: Why do I see that as a massive rationalization?

KAREN: Because that is the way you want to see it. Explanations can be made for scientific errors in the past, and for errors in religion and Christian doctrine. You just have to learn and improve and move on.

PAUL: So all of that bad stuff was in the past. Christianity has learned and moved on. Let's assume that's true. Are you comfortable with all current Christian doctrines?

KAREN: Is this a trick question?

PAUL: Not really. I just want to get you ready for my two biggest objections to your Christian faith.

KAREN: I appreciate the warning. I'll take them one at a time.

PAUL: All right. The first one starts with a lake of fire.

KAREN: Go ahead, but first I think I'll order some ice water.

PAUL: Very funny.

***

A Deep Dark Hole

KAREN: Tell me about this lake of fire you feel so strongly about.

PAUL: I would expect you to feel strongly about it too. How can you worship a God who burns people in an endless fire? Even Hitler didn't do that. He just killed a few million people and burned them in ovens. But that kind of carnage is too mild for your God. He wants to keep people weeping and gnashing their teeth for eternity.

KAREN: Once again I'm afraid you have reached a conclusion based on false evidence.

PAUL: Once again I'm afraid we have stumbled upon two contradictory facts that cannot both be true.

KAREN: What contradictory facts?

PAUL: A forgiving God and eternal punishment. Both can't be true.

KAREN: It depends on what you mean by eternal punishment.

PAUL: You know what I mean. Pain that lasts forever. Bodies burning in fire that never ends. Kung Fu movies on TV twenty-four hours a day. You have heard of Hell, I presume?

KAREN: I have.

PAUL: That is where God sends all the people he loves so much when they break some arbitrary rule, or happen to be born a Hindu. How could you believe in a God who creates a place like that?

KAREN: You've thrown a lot at me. Let me take it a step at a time. First of all, Hell is not a place of eternal torture.

PAUL: Then a lot of kids have been scared to death in Sunday School for nothing.

KAREN: I don't know if it was for nothing—but was probably for the wrong thing.

PAUL: So Hell is not a bad place? You must have read a different Bible than I did.

KAREN: I'm sure it was the same one, but we probably opened it with different goals in mind.

PAUL: How is that?

KAREN: If you already had an image of Hell as a lake of fire, with Satan in a red suit and a pitchfork, you probably found enough in the Bible to support your belief.

PAUL: Wait a minute. Didn't Jesus describe Hell as a lake of fire?

KAREN: Yes he did. He also described it as eternal darkness. Does that seem like a contradiction to you?

PAUL: Yes it does. I don't see how it helps your case to show that Jesus contradicted himself.

KAREN: That is one of the differences between you and me. I don't see the two descriptions as contradictions. I see them as two sides of a colorful metaphor.

PAUL: I hate metaphors. If Jesus wanted to make a point about Hell, why didn't he just come out and say what he meant?

KAREN: Maybe he expected us to be bright enough to think for ourselves. I think Jesus had high expectations for us. Nobody rises to low expectations.

PAUL: You sound like a high school football coach.

KAREN: No one ever accused me of that before.

PAUL: How do you like it?

KAREN: Not so much.

PAUL: Then get back to the subject at hand. If Hell is not a lake of fire, and not eternal darkness, then what is it?

KAREN: I don't know if I can give you a definite answer. Frankly, I am struggling a bit with how to define Hell myself. There is controversy about Hell even among theologians, with a couple of popular views. The most prevalent is that Hell is something as bad as a lake of fire, but worse. It is total separation from God.

PAUL: You continually surprise me with your ability to state the obscure. How is that Hell?

KAREN: Proponents of this view say the Bible makes it clear that people in Hell are full of anguish because they have seen the glory of God, and are banished from his presence. They are banished from any real virtues of any kind. They realize they had a lifetime to turn to God, and they rejected him. Now they get to spend eternity without the only thing that really matters.

PAUL: And that is God?

KAREN: God in all his glory. Love, joy, beauty, fulfillment. God offers all these as a gift. If you reject them, he will honor that choice.

PAUL: Are you saying people choose to go to Hell?

KAREN: They don't consciously choose Hell, I suppose, but by they make that choice by their actions. They choose to reject God. And God respects our choices enough to let us make them, good or bad.

PAUL: If God loves us so much, and wants to keep us out of Hell, why doesn't he make it easier to believe in him? Why doesn't he give us a sign or something?

KAREN: He came to earth and died on the cross for you. Isn't that a sign?

PAUL: That was a long time ago. Where is the message for our time?

KAREN: I don't see how you could improve on the message he already sent. Besides, our record for listening isn't that good. God sent countless prophets to tell us the story. We stoned them. He became a man himself. We killed him. There are churches in every town. Bibles in every library. Evangelists on TV and radio. If you don't meet God in our time, it is because you are running away from him. And by doing that, you sprint into Hell.

PAUL: If Hell exists.

KAREN: If Hell exits. You remind me of the story of John Colter.

PAUL: John Colter. Wasn't he a Mountain Man? Part of the Lewis and Clark expedition?

KAREN: Right. Blackfeet Indians captured him, stripped him naked, and let him have a running head start before they took off after him.

PAUL: With evil intentions, no doubt.

KAREN: No doubt. But Colter fooled them. He outran them for a while, and then dove in a creek, where he hid in a beaver hut until the Blackfeet gave up the search.

PAUL: A beaver hut is something a beaver lives in?

KAREN: It's like a condo built of sticks and leaves.

PAUL: Sounds lovely, but I don't see how it proves the existence of Hell.

KAREN: Stay with me for a minute. John Colter was hundreds of miles from any kind of help when he escaped the Blackfeet. He walked barefoot and naked across the mountains to get back to civilization. Guess what he found on the way? Fountains of steam shooting out of the ground, ponds of boiling water, gashes in the earth's crusts with hot, bubbling mud oozing out. He told the other mountain men about the place when he made it back to civilization. They thought he was crazy. They called the place "Colter's Hell." Thought it was just a bad dream.

PAUL: I know how this story ends. Colter's Hell was Yellowstone Park. I'm still waiting for the lesson.

KAREN: Nobody believed John Colter. Nobody believed in Colter's Hell. But it was there, just the same. Not unlike the Hell we've been talking about. Whether you choose to believe it or not, it is there.

PAUL: Colter walked naked through his Hell. Nobody has even seen yours. You believe in Hell because the Bible says it's true, and the Bible is true because the Bible says so. Your reasoning is circular.

KAREN: I think my reasoning is more of a straight line. We already talked about why the four gospels are reliable. We discussed why I believe Jesus was God in human form. If both those statements are true, then I would be foolish not to believe what Jesus said. And like it or not, Jesus taught there is a Hell, and it is a place to be avoided.

PAUL: Maybe not. You say there is no torture and no flames. Maybe Hell is not so bad. I'm sure there are some interesting people there.

KAREN: That sort of thinking can get you in trouble. The Hell we have been talking about is an awful place, full of self-centered people and the agony of what might have been. No love, no beauty, no joy.

PAUL: That sounds like a weekend at my grand-mother's house.

KAREN: How would you like to spend eternity there?

PAUL: I have. Several times. But I think I picked up a little doubt in your voice. What do you mean by the phrase "the Hell we have been talking about?" Is there a different Hell than the one we have been talking about?

KAREN: There is another view of Hell that has been gaining popularity in the last few years. You may like it. It actually has that lake of fire you are so fond of.

PAUL: Oh sure. People are thrown into fire to burn in agony for eternity? Never any rest. Never any relief. Have you touched a hot skillet? Or burned your hand with scalding water? Would you inflict that on some-one forever? I wouldn't do that to Hitler. I wouldn't do that to a rat or a snake. Yet your God does it to innocent children who never heard of Him. That is quite a God you worship.

KAREN: You are jumping ahead of me. I said this view of Hell includes a lake of fire. I did not say people are in it for eternity.

PAUL: What do they do? Camp on the beach?

KAREN: They are thrown in the fire and destroyed. Body and soul.

PAUL: Destroyed? What about the immortal soul the Bible talks about?

KAREN: The Bible never says that humans are immortal. It does say that God can grant eternal life through Jesus, but that doesn't mean that everyone on earth is immortal.

PAUL: I am trying to not let this confuse me. Let's focus. Where do you get the idea that souls are destroyed in Hell? I thought you Christians believed in everlasting punishment.

KAREN: Punishment can be a single event to a single person. The fact that it is everlasting could just mean that it is always occurring to someone, but not eternally to the same one.

PAUL: You might get hung as a heretic for talking like this. Christians love to scare people with eternity in Hell.

KAREN: It seems to me this eternal torture thing is a man-made concept. The Bible clearly states in several places that the wages of sin is death, and that we don't need to fear those who can kill the body but not the

180

soul. That tells me the soul can be destroyed. And if it is destroyed, it is not in Hell.

PAUL: So Hell is either eternal torture or eternal destruction. Either way, I don't see how you can be comfortable with that scary little chunk of Christian doctrine.

KAREN: Frankly, I don't like the idea of Hell. It is very, very sad. But there is a difference between something I don't like and something I don't believe.

PAUL: But if you don't like it, and you see how terrible it is, how can you believe your loving God allows it?

KAREN: Because I can see, intellectually, that it makes sense.

PAUL: You may have to explain that to me.

KAREN: Look at it this way. Hell is the ultimate compliment God pays to us. He respects our choices so much that he will not force us to make the one he would prefer.

PAUL: That is a pretty twisted compliment. I think I would rather be insulted a little, and end up in heaven.

KAREN: Maybe I didn't phrase that the way I should have. God cannot give us the free will to make choices and then force us to choose him. We were created to love him and love each other. We can choose not to do either. He will let us.

PAUL: I don't think it's that simple. Going to Hell is not all our choice. God has rules. At least ten of them. If we don't follow the rules, he sends us to Hell.

KAREN: There are rules to live by, that's true. You sound like that's a problem for you.

PAUL: I don't see why there have to be rules and restrictions. Why can't we just live the way we want to?

KAREN: You know better than that. Why do you even ask a question that silly?

PAUL: What is silly about it? I say, the more personal freedom, the better.

KAREN: Personal freedom has to be restrained by some kind of rules, just to maintain order. What do you think would happen if there were no rules or restrictions in a football game?

PAUL: It would be a high scoring game.

KAREN: How do you know there would be a score? How can you score if there are no rules to define a touchdown?

182

PAUL: OK. I don't want to ruin the Super Bowl. Let football have its rules. But give me my personal freedom.

KAREN: Do you think your life would improve if there were no rules to live by?

PAUL: It might be fun to find out.

KAREN: Or it might not. Tell me, how would you enjoy the world with no rules against rape, or murder, or theft, or drunken driving, or assault and battery?

PAUL: What neighborhood do you think I live in?

KAREN: It doesn't matter. If you eliminate the rules, society degenerates quickly into chaos.

PAUL: All right. I'll admit some rules are necessary. But I don't see why God sends us to Hell if we disobey them. That sounds like a two-year-old throwing a tantrum when he doesn't get his way.

KAREN: As I said, it's not like you don't have a choice. You don't accidentally murder somebody, or steal a car. You don't accidentally lie to your friends, or gossip, or steal an ice cream cone.

PAUL: Hey, I was only thirteen when I took that ice cream. I don't think you were going to eat it anyway.

KAREN: I don't hold grudges. I forgave you a long time ago.

PAUL: Then you must be a better person than God. God doesn't forgive. He has this gaping hole for us to fall into if we don't fit his idea of perfection.

KAREN: God can forgive, and wants to. But he won't force forgiveness on you if you don't want it.

PAUL: Who wouldn't want forgiveness if it means dodging Hell?

KAREN: It all comes back to choices. If you choose to reject God, and ignore his rules, and live your life with yourself as the center of the universe, then you have no right to expect forgiveness. You had your whole life to make the right choice. If you didn't, that is not God's fault.

PAUL: Doesn't that strike you as a little harsh?

KAREN: Is it harsh for a bank to bounce your check if you have no money in your account?

PAUL: Have you been looking at my bank statements?

KAREN: They are probably in better shape than mine.

PAUL: Being broke is kind of a Hell, isn't it?

KAREN: A moderate version, I guess.

PAUL: Moderate or severe, the point of Hell eludes me. I just don't see the justification.

KAREN: Hell is one part of God's creation that gives our lives meaning.

PAUL: You are getting obscure again.

KAREN: I'll try to make myself clearer. Do you remember the project we worked on in Ethics class for Dr. Claude?

PAUL: That was a pretty good imitation of Hell. I don't remember it giving my life meaning.

KAREN: Neither do I. And I'll tell you why. We worked on that project for weeks. Interviewed people, did research all night, rewrote it a dozen times. We wanted to have the best project in the class, remember?

PAUL: It was the best in the class.

KAREN: It probably was. But what did "Dr. Death" do with the grades?

PAUL: He gave everybody in the class an A.

KAREN: Right. He didn't even read the reports. Didn't even look at them. He just gave everybody an A, and acted like he was doing us a favor. I was furious.

PAUL: You were less than forgiving at that time, I recall. You wouldn't even shake his hand at the end of the course.

KAREN: That was petty, all right, but I was pretty worked up. Don't you see why? He completely trivialized all of our hard work. We deserved some recognition. We deserved to have our worked judged, good or bad. By giving everybody an A, he made all of our work and dedication meaningless.

PAUL: I suppose he did. But he didn't keep us in that condition for eternity. We eventually escaped his evil clutches and put him behind us. At least I did.

KAREN: I'm working on it.

PAUL: It's good to see you grow as a person. It's not healthy to hold on to unpleasant memories. Especially for God, I would think. But he condemns people to Hell for eternity. Or annihilates them. I don't know which is worse.

KAREN: I told you I don't like the idea of Hell. But I have to accept it as true, and make the best of it.

186

PAUL: That can't be too easy. Especially if you consider the majority of people who will be doomed to go there.

KAREN: Who is that?

PAUL: The millions, or billions of people on earth who have never heard of Jesus Christ. All of the devout Buddhists, or Hindus, even Jews. It seems to me Hell must be overflowing with a lot of very disappointed holy men.

KAREN: I can only give you my opinion on that. The Bible says Jesus is the only way to God. He is the way to eternal salvation. So I know if I turn to Jesus I will be saved. I don't know what will happen to the holy men and women of other religions who worship another God. I suspect their afterlife won't be as pleasant as mine.

PAUL: Do you mean they will go to Hell because they didn't preach the blood of Jesus on Sundays?

KAREN: I think there are different levels of punishment, and different levels of reward. They may be at a different level than followers of Christ.

PAUL: So you are superior to them?

KAREN: Hardly. I am as big a sinner as anybody. But I chose to follow the path to God as he laid it out.

PAUL: And the people who have never heard of Jesus?

KAREN: I don't know. I do know that God is just. I can't imagine that when I hear the answer to your question I will be disappointed.

PAUL: Your take on Hell seems a bit vague to me. Why is that?

KAREN: To tell you the truth, I don't think about it all that much, since I have no intention of ending up there. If I am going on vacation in Hawaii, I don't spend all my time thinking about how terrible things are in Haiti.

PAUL: That is fine for you, but you have to agree that the idea of Hell is quite an obstacle to faith for unbelievers.

KAREN: I certainly agree with that. But you can't make your decision about faith in God based on one issue. If you look at the overall picture, your decision will be different.

PAUL: Now you sound like a politician.

KAREN: Is that better than a football coach, or worse?

PAUL: That depends on the politician. I have another question for you. If you can answer this one, I'll go put on sackcloth and ashes.

KAREN: I don't think they allow that in the coffee shop.

***

Pain Hurts

PAUL: I saved my best question for last. Prepare to be overwhelmed. Are you ready?

KAREN: I was born ready, baby sister, and I intend to go out that way.

PAUL: You've been watching John Wayne movies again, haven't you?

KAREN: <u>True Grit</u>. Rooster Cogburn talking to Mattie Ross, before they saddle up to chase down Lucky Ned Pepper.

PAUL: Fascinating.

KAREN: I guess we can discuss the nuances of a John Wayne movie at another time.

PAUL: It might be a short discussion.

KAREN: Fair enough. Let me have your overwhelming question.

PAUL: It has several parts. You say there is a loving God, right?

KAREN: That is what I say.

PAUL: And this God of yours is all powerful?

KAREN: All powerful.

PAUL: And your God wants the best for us, right? He wants to take care of us, right?

KAREN: Why do I feel like I'm a mouse, and you just tossed out a bit of cheese?

PAUL: Because I am about to spring the trap. Answer this, if you can: If God is all powerful, all loving, and wants our lives to be good, then why is there evil and suffering in the world?

KAREN: Do you think there is a contradiction hidden there somewhere?

PAUL: Are you kidding? It's about as hidden as a house on fire. An all powerful God who allows evil and suffering is not a loving God. A loving God who cannot stop evil and suffering is not all powerful. Since evil and suffering exist, your loving and all powerful God cannot.

KAREN: Cannot? Without question? Are you certain of that?

PAUL: Only if the rules of logic apply. The rules you love to use when it proves your point.

KAREN: I love logic. But it has its limitations.

PAUL: It is interesting that you find them now, when it works against you.

KAREN: You are trying to use logic outside of its limits.

PAUL: So you keep saying. What limits are you talking about?

KAREN: It's simple. Man created logic to understand what goes on around him. He can do that when he has adequate information. I don't know if we have adequate information about why God allows suffering.

PAUL: That is too easy. You use logic when it works for you. When it doesn't, you say it can't be applied. That is phony reasoning.

KAREN: Logic works when we understand the theory we are trying to explain. I don't know if we understand God's purpose for suffering well enough to draw a conclusion.

PAUL: You disappoint me. My objection against your God makes perfect sense. You respond with an argument so weak it's insulting.

KAREN: Let me try to strengthen my argument. Would you say there is a big difference between my dog Ruby and me?

PAUL: Ruby walks on four legs. But I can make that observation without logic.

KAREN: My point is that there is a big difference between Ruby and me, just as there is a big difference between God and me.

PAUL: Let's hope so.

KAREN: It's a safe bet. So I will probably understand God's methods no better than Ruby understands mine.

PAUL: I thought you told me God was knowable. Now you can't understand him?

KAREN: God is knowable. But he wouldn't be much of a God if I could understand everything about him. It would be like Ruby understanding everything about me. Let me give you an example. If I try to remove a splinter from Ruby's paw, she will try to pull it away. She might even snap at me. The more I dig around in her paw, the more it hurts. Ruby would only experience the pain. She couldn't understand that I was trying to help her.

PAUL: Are you saying God is a splinter in the paw of life?

KAREN: Not exactly. But how do we know the suffering we experience in life isn't God trying to remove a splinter? Maybe suffering is His way of teaching us life's lessons. It's like a lump of coal. It doesn't turn into a diamond until it's put under pressure. We may not fully develop until we suffer.

PAUL: So when our friend Andy died in that car crash, and left Julie with two little kids and no life insurance, that was God teaching her a lesson? Then your God is a fiend.

KAREN: I won't try to discount the tragedy Julie experienced. But I can't draw the conclusion that nothing good can come from it. I am not wise enough to know that. God may use it to his good purpose.

PAUL: I don't see how that helps Julie pay her mortgage. Or keeps her kids from crying themselves to sleep every night because their daddy is gone. Your lack of sympathy angers me, to tell you the truth.

KAREN: Don't accuse me of lacking sympathy. It breaks my heart to see Julie and the kids suffer like that.

It's just that, rationally, I can understand there may be something good happening behind the scenes.

PAUL: Something good. Right. Like when my father died two years ago from lung cancer. There was a great piece of God's planning for you. Everybody who knew my Dad loved him. He painted cars for a living, and didn't leave his neighborhood for years, so he was hardly a famous man. But there were so many people at his funeral that traffic was tied up for blocks. Everybody loved him. You knew him. You know what he was like. My Dad was the best man I ever knew. And God killed him before he was sixty. How does that turn coal into diamonds?

KAREN: I have to tread softly here. I have to give you an answer you won't like.

PAUL: Be careful.

KAREN: Both the examples you gave are the result of bad choices. Free will gone bad.

PAUL: My dad chose to die at age 55? Andy chose to die in a car crash and leave his kids fatherless? What the Hell are you talking about?

KAREN: I'm talking about the fact that Andy chose to drink beer all afternoon and then drive home. He rolled his car because he was too drunk to operate a car. I don't think his kids can blame God for that. Their suffering is a result of the bad choice Andy made.

PAUL: That is cold-blooded.

KAREN: Truth often is.

PAUL: I suppose you have some truth about my Dad.

KAREN: I think it's a truth you already know. Your dad smoked cigars and chewed tobacco every waking moment of his adult life. God didn't make him do that. He chose to. And the tobacco gave him cancer. Not God.

PAUL: But this all powerful God could have saved him. My mother's church prayed for him for months. Where was God then? Why didn't he intervene to save my Dad? Wasn't that allowing my suffering? And my mother's?

KAREN: Your father made his choice, and God respected it. It was a bad choice, just as Andy's was. Both were contrary to God's plan, or God's wishes. When you make choices like that, you open yourself up to bad results. Much of the suffering in the world is caused by human choices, not God's will.

PAUL: I don't find that particularly comforting. Or convincing. Your god could still stop the suffering, and he doesn't.

KAREN: Look at it this way. If he did stop all the suffering, there would be no free will. People could not make choices. We would be machines. By giving us the gift of choice, God had to give us the ability to make bad choices.

PAUL: Some people make bad choices. Maybe in your god's world they have to pay for them. When does God pay for his choices?

KAREN: I don't see what you mean.

PAUL: If God created everything, and evil exists in the world, then God created evil. That doesn't make him a loving god, it makes him a monster.

KAREN: God did not create evil.

PAUL: But you told me he created everything. Of course, an all knowing, all powerful, loving God wouldn't create evil—but evil exists. Will you agree that evil exists?

KAREN: No question. Evil exists.

PAUL: And your loving god exists?

KAREN: He does.

PAUL: Then how does that fit your idea of truth? You told me earlier that two facts that contradict each other cannot both be true. I just described the ultimate contradiction. A loving god who creates evil? It cannot be. If God created evil, then he must be evil himself.

KAREN: Your original premise is wrong. Evil certainly exists. No one could doubt that. God exists as well. But God did not create evil. He created the possibility of evil. By giving us free will, he gave us the ability to choose evil.

PAUL: But he could stop it. He could intervene at any time. If he was a good, loving god, he would protect us a little bit.

KAREN: He protects us a lot. But you have to admit that personal growth often comes out of suffering, or evil circumstances. If God spared us all of our pain, he would deprive us of much of our pleasure. It's like when my Dad taught me to ride a bike. I didn't want him to let go of the bike, because I fell down a lot. It hurt. But if he didn't let go, I would never learn to ride. Maybe God works the same way. He lets us suffer so we can learn. Maybe so we can experience more joy later.

PAUL: Tell that to my mother. Tell that to Julie. Try to tell them their lives were ruined so they could learn a life lesson. Your condescending attitude drives me crazy. You trivialize all the pain and suffering in the world when you say it is for our own good, or because we made bad choices. You have no evidence for your position. It is all theory and supposition. And it is cold-blooded as Hell.

KAREN: I apologize if I appear to minimize your pain. I know it is real.

PAUL: Apology accepted. But let's look at this from a different angle. How do you explain the problem of evil to Matt? His son developed leukemia at six years of age. Did he choose that? Was that six-year-old being punished for bad choices? How about Robert's little brother? He was run over by a rock truck while Robert stood in his front yard and watched it happen. What part of God's plan included wrapping that little boy's body around the driveshaft? Whose choices caused that God-allowed incident? Who got turned into a diamond that day?

KAREN: I wish I could answer that.

PAUL: I wish you could too. I'm sure Matt does too, as he takes his son for chemotherapy, and watches his little boy's hair fall out, and watches him puke all over the kitchen floor every time he takes a treatment. You're awfully fond of the Bible story. Where did Jesus explain all this to us? Where did he explain the need for suffering?

KAREN: Nowhere I can find. Jesus didn't tell us why we would have so much pain and strife, but he made it very clear we would. I don't know why. Maybe we couldn't handle it if we knew. All I know is that he said we would have a lot of trouble in this world, but we should take heart and be of good cheer.

PAUL: Why?

KAREN: Because Jesus has overcome this world. He is our great hope, because he is there for us. We will never be alone or forsaken. We will always have a friend and a comforter.

PAUL: I'm glad you find that so reassuring, but wouldn't you like to know for certain why God allows all the pain in the world?

KAREN: Yes I would. I can try my best to defend the rationale behind suffering, but that doesn't make it a whole lot easier to experience. And I know my reasoning would sound trivial and trite to anyone in the midst of real pain, like Matt or Julie. But the fact that I have a hard time dealing with human suffering doesn't mean there is no reason for it.

PAUL: That is not good enough for me. I want an answer.

KAREN: I can't disagree with you on that. I would like an answer too. So would most people, I suppose.

PAUL: I don't see us getting one any time soon.

KAREN: That reminds me of a church service I saw broadcast on television shortly after the 9/11 attacks on the World Trade Center. Maybe you saw it. The service was at the National Cathedral in Washington, D.C. The great evangelist Billy Graham spoke that day. He knew people would ask "Why?" He knew they would want to know why God would allow such an evil act to occur. Reverend Graham's answer, as best I can remember it, came down to this: "I don't know why such evil exists. We may never know until we reach heaven and speak to God. But I know that we have hope in troubled times. We have hope in Jesus."

PAUL: I wish I could take as much comfort in that as you do. I'm not sure hope in Jesus trumps the pain and suffering in the world. It is hard for me to worship a god who allows all this pain.

KAREN: I am not convinced that we would be better off without the suffering. I know that seems like nonsense to you, but I believe it is true.

PAUL: Seems? I know not "seems." I know what it is. It is cold and mean. It's like God is so removed from our suffering that he isn't affected by it, so he allows it to continue.

KAREN: You need to remember that Jesus suffered too. God knows what suffering is like. He knows hunger, fatigue, rejection, torture, and death. There is no pain we can feel that Jesus didn't feel. I wish I knew more about why pain is necessary. I don't know. I wish I could handle it better. I can't. But I do know Jesus is with us, and that makes it bearable. He won't leave us alone. Jesus is like a friend when you are sick or hurting. He will be there for you.

PAUL: Do you mean he will be there for people in general, or do you mean me specifically?

KAREN: He is a big God. He can be there for me and you. God loves you.

PAUL: I wish he would show it a little more often.

KAREN: Maybe we can arrange that.

***

Not Today

PAUL: You're not going to preach a sermon are you?

KAREN: I'm not qualified for that.

PAUL: It seems to me you came pretty close today.

KAREN: I wasn't trying to preach. But I can't listen to criticisms of my beliefs without making some kind of response.

PAUL: You can't watch Bugs Bunny without making some kind of response, but you seemed to feel a special need to challenge me on this topic. How come?

KAREN: Because I thought that was the best way to open your mind to the possibilities. If I would have walked in the coffee shop singing hymns and quoting scripture, I doubt if our conversation would have lasted long.

PAUL: I would have taken my latte to go. I've heard you sing.

KAREN: Thanks for that boost to my self-esteem.

PAUL: My pleasure. Why are you trying to open my mind to the possibilities of your God anyway?

KAREN: What kind of friend would I be if I didn't? If I saw the best movie ever, wouldn't you want me to tell you about it? What kind of friend would I be if I knew about an investment that would guarantee a tremendous return on your money, and I kept it to myself?

PAUL: Is that how you feel about your God talk?

KAREN: That is how I feel about God. Human language is inadequate to describe what you can get from a relationship with God. Everlasting life, peace, joy, truth, meaning, fellowship with a family of believers.

PAUL: I think your human language is holding its own. But I went to Bible school with you when we were kids. I don't remember you rhapsodizing over God then.

KAREN: I didn't then. Until recently, I was stuck in Plato's cave.

PAUL: That sounds familiar. Refresh my memory.

KAREN: The Greek philosopher Plato told the story—or allegory, really—of men chained in a cave, with their backs to the entrance. The sun was outside, but they never saw it. The only thing they could see were shadows on the cave wall, so they believed the shadows were all there was to reality. One of them escaped the cave, but the sun was so painful to look at, he shielded his eyes and turned away at first. But once he opened his eyes, he came to love the light, and never wanted to go back into the darkness.

PAUL: Why didn't he go back to help his buddies?

KAREN: You remind me a lot of Plato. He did go back, but no one believed his stories. They were so accustomed to darkness they had no desire to look towards the light. They couldn't even believe it was real. So they stayed in the dark.

PAUL: So now you are out of the cave, basking in the sun, and I am stuck in the dark, too afraid to look at the light.

KAREN: It is almost poetic, isn't it?

PAUL: If it is true, it is a tragedy. If it is not, it is a farce.

KAREN: It doesn't have to be either. The curtain hasn't come down yet. There is still time to change the ending of your personal drama.

PAUL: I'm still curious about what caused the change in you.

KAREN: It was a long time coming. I was introduced to Christianity the same way you were. I was forced to go to church on Sundays and Bible School in the summer. All I saw in it was boring hymns, rules and ritual. Even the adults didn't seem to be having a good time, but if I missed a Sunday, they would stop me on the street to ask why I wasn't there. I thought they should mind their own business. I got so disgusted that I stopped going altogether.

PAUL: We are on the same track so far. What happened next?

KAREN: I started searching for something to believe in. I felt there was something out there I was missing. So I read Greek philosophy, Buddhism, Indian gurus, New Age spiritualism, you name it. I felt like I was getting close, but there was still something missing. Then I worked one summer directing traffic on a construction job. I met an ex-Marine whose hobby had been picking fights in bars on weekends. He told me Jesus saved his life. I thought I knew enough about Jesus, so I shrugged it off. Then I worked evenings for a while in a warehouse. The guy in charge of freight was a part-time pastor. He told me how Jesus had saved him from drowning himself in booze. That is when I started to read the Bible. I found out there was a lot about Jesus they didn't bother to bring up in that old church.

PAUL: So reading the Bible was all it took to convert you?

KAREN: No. Like I said earlier, I was not exactly a willing convert. I thought you had to be pretty stupid to believe all those Christian myths. Reading the Bible started to change my mind. What finally pushed me over the edge was a book by C. S. Lewis, called <u>Mere Christianity</u>. It was so logical, so reasonable, and so obviously true, that I had to look further. I devoured books on Christian apologetics.

PAUL: Apologetics?

KAREN: That means a defense of an opinion or belief. Christian apologetics are a defense of the Christian faith.

PAUL: Are these books on apologetics where you got the information you attacked me with today?

KAREN: Most of it.

PAUL: Maybe I should read some of those books.

KAREN: I'd be glad to give you a reading list.

PAUL: I'll take a look at it. Tell me, has becoming a Christian really made a difference in your life?

KAREN: You know it has. My attitude toward life changed completely. I used to be so cocky and argumentative that people couldn't stand to be around me.

After I found Jesus, somebody asked me if I was taking tranquilizers, because I seemed so happy all the time.

PAUL: I'm not sure that even Jesus can stop you from arguing. Are you telling me that you are happy all the time?

KAREN: Not all the time. But when I get frustrated or angry, or even depressed, I know I have someone to turn to. I can't stay down for long. It is hard to be an unhappy Christian.

PAUL: Why is that? Does Jesus solve all of your problems?

KAREN: No. Christians have the same problems as everybody else. They just have a different perspective on them. The problems of this life become less critical when viewed in the light of eternity.

PAUL: How about life's pleasures? I suspect they diminish as faith increases.

KAREN: Hardly. God invented pleasure. Good food, good company, music, dancing. God invented them all. Jesus said he came that we might have an abundant life. I think God wants us to enjoy ourselves.

PAUL: What about sex?

KAREN: God invented that too, and he expects us to enjoy it. Sex can become a sin, just like eating too much, or drinking too much, but if you follow God's plan, pleasures multiply rather than diminish. That has certainly been true in my life.

PAUL: I'm glad that worked out for you. You are quite a salesman for the Almighty, but I don't think your arguments today are enough to convince me I need Jesus.

KAREN: I don't think logical arguments alone can lead anybody to God. They just show that you don't have to be naïve or foolish to be a believer.

PAUL: I guess you win on that point. Christians may not be as intellectually bankrupt as I thought.

KAREN: But you are not persuaded?

PAUL: Almost persuaded.

KAREN: But not quite?

PAUL: Not quite. Which is a shame, really. Sometimes I would like to believe. You have a peace and confidence that I envy. I feel there must be more to life than I have seen so far, and you seem to have found it. But I just can't force myself to make the leap.

KAREN: The leap to faith in Jesus?

PAUL: Right. I'm just not sure.

KAREN: May I make a suggestion?

PAUL: Is there any way to stop you?

KAREN: I know you really want to hear it. I suggest you say the same prayer I did when I wanted to find a way to trust in Jesus. You say a prayer accepting Jesus on faith, and pray that he will reveal himself to you. You ask for forgiveness and invite Jesus into your life.

PAUL: I don't think so. It seems hypocritical to pray to a God that I am not completely convinced exists. You need to accept that fact that some people just don't believe what you do, and aren't interested in changing their minds.

KAREN: Of course I accept it, just like I accept that rain is wet and rocks are hard. But I can't change rain or rocks.

PAUL: Do you think you can change me?

KAREN: With Christ, all things are possible.

PAUL: It's also possible that I'll leave the coffee shop today no farther down the road to faith than when I got here.

KAREN: And it's possible that you are just being stubborn. It is possible that you don't want to admit there is a God because you might have to change some of your behavior. It's possible that you are afraid that I might be right.

PAUL: I am usually afraid that you might be right.

KAREN: Then you need to take a gamble. Think of it this way. If you become a follower of Jesus, and it turns out in the end that I was wrong, you will have really lost nothing in the bargain. If you don't become a follower of Jesus, and it turns out I was right, you will have lost everything. Forever. If you look at it as a risk/benefit issue, this should be the easiest decision you ever make.

PAUL: You should go into sales. You really know how to close a deal.

KAREN: Are you ready to pray for a little personal revelation?

PAUL: Can you do that in public?

KAREN: I did it in front of a dozen people in a church basement. Let me make it easy for you. I'll say the words, and you just repeat them silently to yourself. Let this prayer be your prayer.

PAUL: Wait a minute. You're about to embarrass me. I don't want you praying over me in public. There may be people in here who know me.

KAREN: We don't have to do it here. You can pray on the street, or in an open field, or in the front seat of that little econobox car you drive.

PAUL: It's not enough to call me a heathen. Now you're making fun of my car.

KAREN: Don't be so sensitive. I think your car is cute. Small, but cute. At least listen to the prayer, OK?

PAUL: OK. I'll listen.

KAREN: Dear Heavenly Father, I realize that I'm a sinner. I'm sorry for all the mistakes I've made, and all the things I've done wrong. I ask your forgiveness, and turn away from these things now. I thank you for Jesus' sacrifice on the cross. I know he died for me so that I could be forgiven and released from my sins. I accept Jesus as my Lord and Savior. I pray that as I read your word and meet with your people, you will reveal yourself to me. I ask you to come into my life, and change my life. I ask these things and give thanks in the name of Jesus. Then you say amen.

PAUL: Look. Karen. I know you're my friend. I am, and always will be yours. I know you want the best for me. But you're asking me to make a profession of faith that I don't feel. You've changed my mind about some things today. You've made me curious. I'll tell you what we'll do. You send me your recommended reading list, and I'll read a book or two. Then you can take another shot at me. I promise that I'll pursue this further and talk to you again about it. But I am not accepting Jesus today.

KAREN: That's okay. I wish you had made a different decision, but everybody is at a different place on the path. I just hope I've moved you a little farther in your journey. And I'll do better than send you a list. I'll send you a couple of books—with highlights and notations.

PAUL: Highlights and notations. You'll be prodding me along even when you're not in the room. You are quite a piece of work. How about this, though? I'll send you a book to read, and we can compare notes afterwards. Fair enough?

KAREN: Sounds like a challenge for both of us.

PAUL: I think you're up to it. And who knows? I may become a preacher someday, just because of you. But right now we need to get out of here before they throw us out.

KAREN: Let me pay for the sandwiches and coffee.

PAUL: No. No. Let me get it.

KAREN: Really?

PAUL: I insist.

KAREN: You are changing already.

PAUL: Not that much. Get the tip.

***

The Books

Karen's Books

Alpha: Questions of Life, by Nicky Gumbel

Mere Christianity, by C. S. Lewis

Paul's Book

The God Delusion, by Richard Dawkins

***

About the Author

In the journey that led me to this book, I spent time as a university instructor, a salesman, an industrial plant manager, an electrician, a pipe-layer, an agnostic, a confused searcher, and a reluctant believer. I traveled to over forty states, Mexico, Canada, Central America, the Caribbean, and Western Europe. Searching, talking, listening.

No one could have predicted that I would become a university instructor or a Christian author. My father was a construction worker, and my mother an atheist. Both expected me to follow in their footsteps, and for a good part of my life, I did. I spent too many years earning my rent with a strong back and a shovel. When a frigid Nebraska winter forced me underground to work in a warm, fragrant sewer, I began to see the benefit of a college degree.

My journey to faith was even longer, filled with detours and dead ends. I dabbled in philosophy, flirted with New Age mysticism, even read the New Testament from cover to cover with an eye toward rebuttal. Nothing resonated. Then I attended a twelve-week class called Alpha; an Introduction to Christianity.

As a result of that class, I absorbed books on Christian apologetics, facilitated classes on the Christian faith, spoke before groups interested in evangelism, and taught Sunday School classes for high school students.

Those students inspired me to write this book. All of the students were "good Christians." Most were going off to college soon. But as disheartening as it may be from a Christian perspective, none could convincingly answer the basic question, "Why do you believe what you believe?" I developed lessons to teach them how to answer the questions they would inevitably be asked when they reached college. Those lessons evolved into God and Other Things.

Let me know what you think. If you would like to write a review of the book, or just post a comment, please find the book at http://www.amazon.com/. You can also visit my website at GodandOtherThings.org.

***